MW01713885

Art Therapy

COLORING BOOK

Menagerie & More

hinkler

Published by Hinkler Books Pty Ltd
45–55 Fairchild Street
Heatherton Victoria 3202 Australia
www.hinkler.com.au

Cover design: Poo a Desai
Internal design: Aimee Zumis
Illustrators: Smiljana Coh and Patricia McCarthy
Prepress: Graphic Print Group

ISBN: 978 1 4889 0286 4

Printed and bound in USA

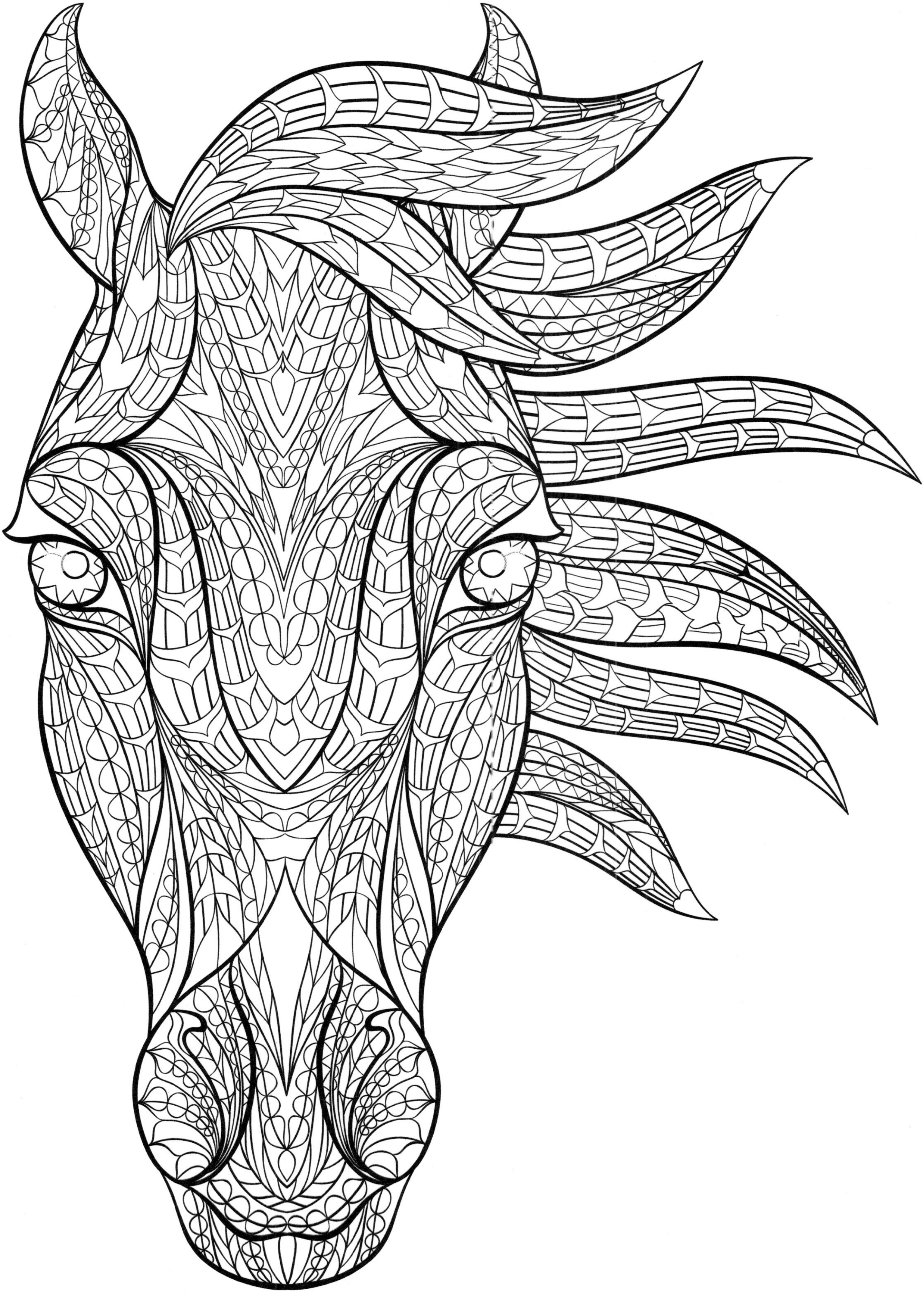

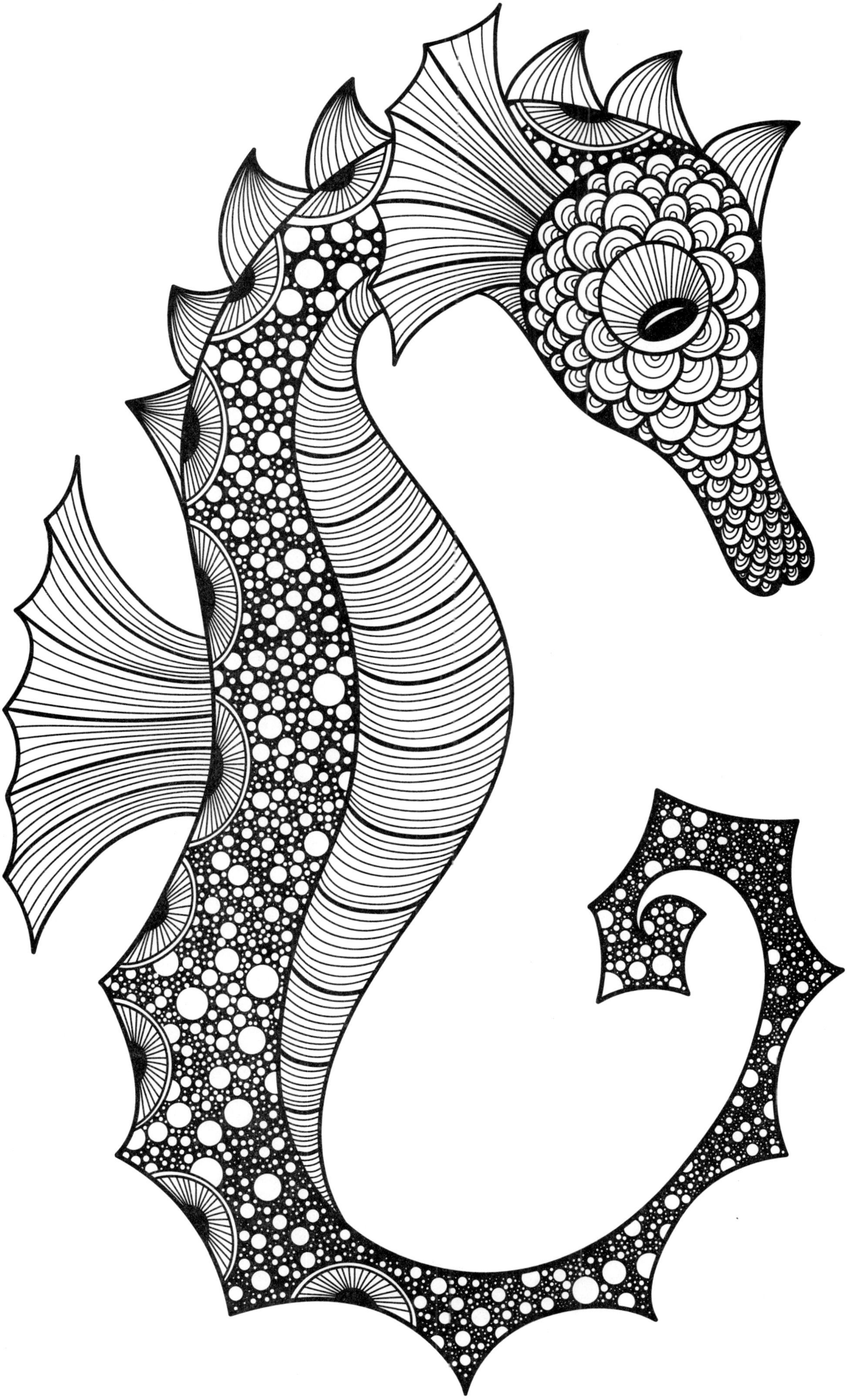

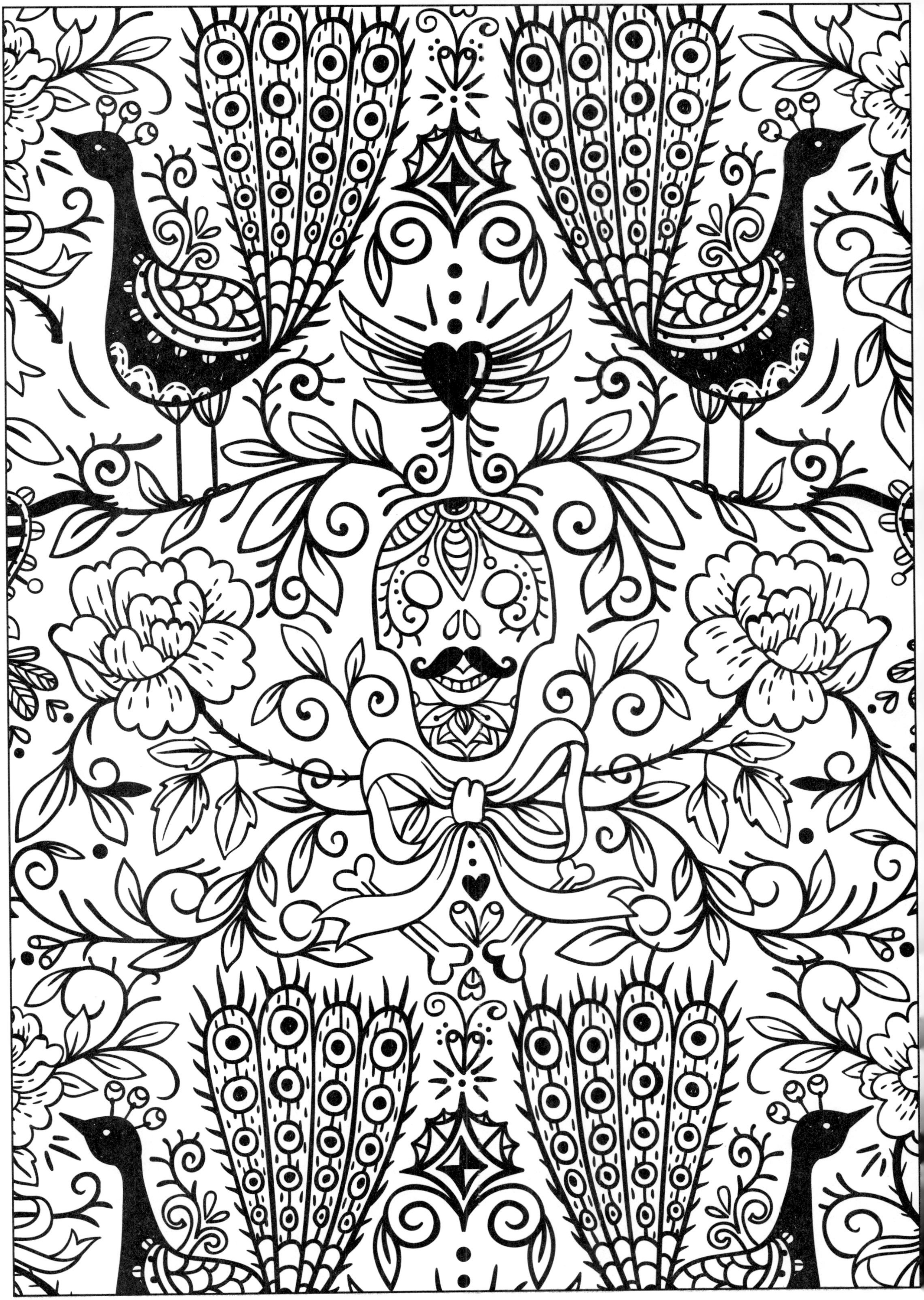

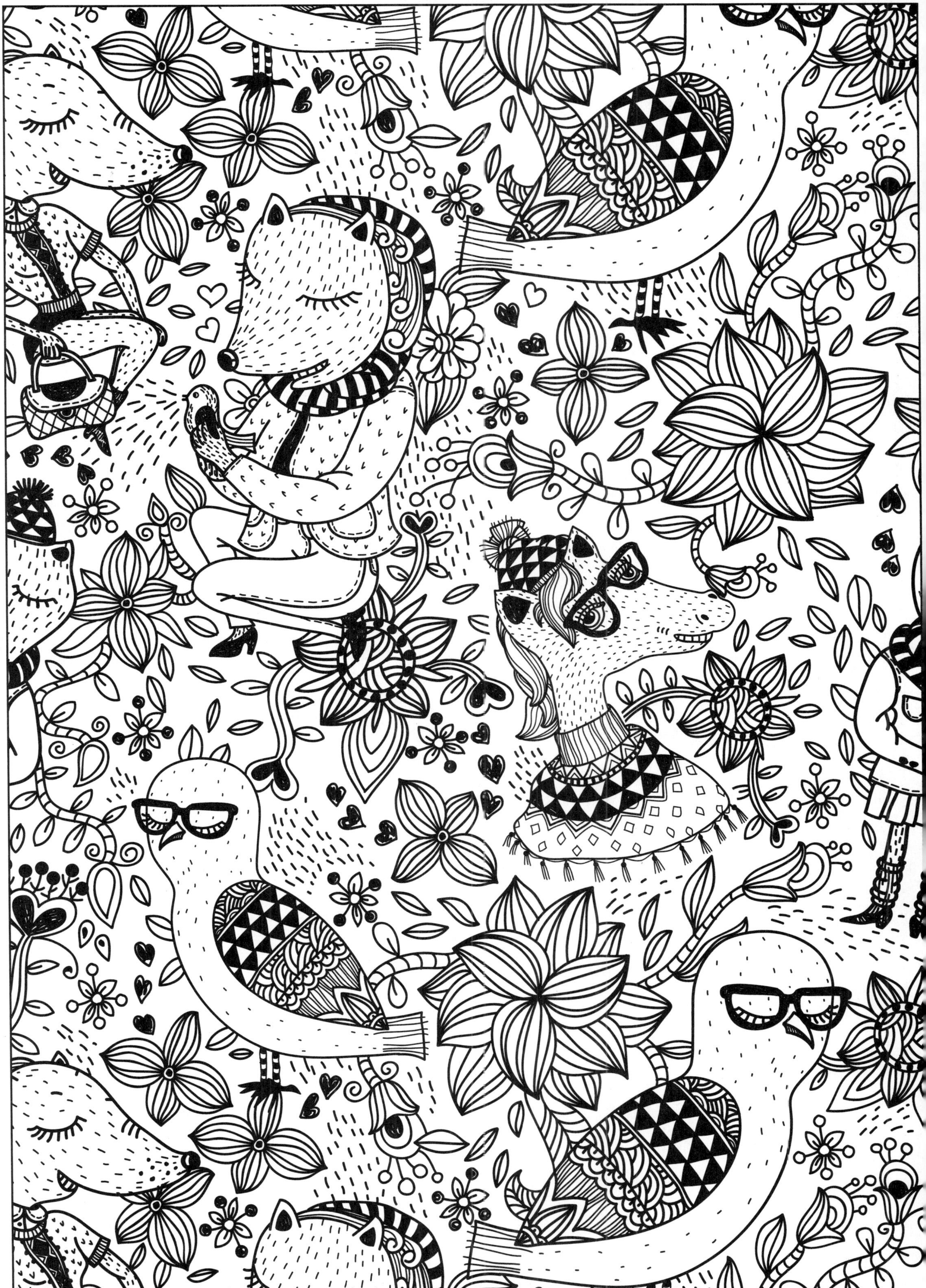

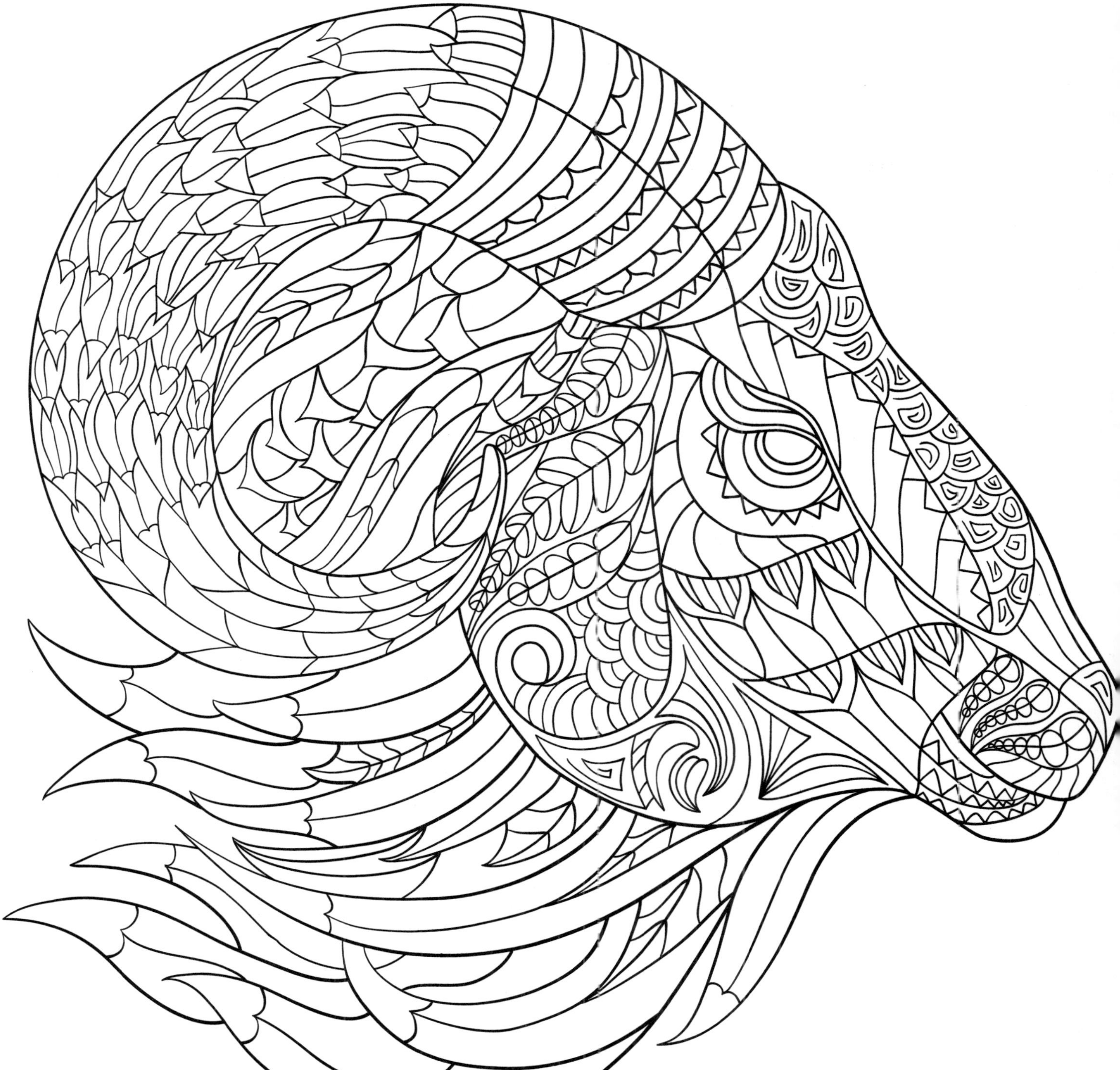

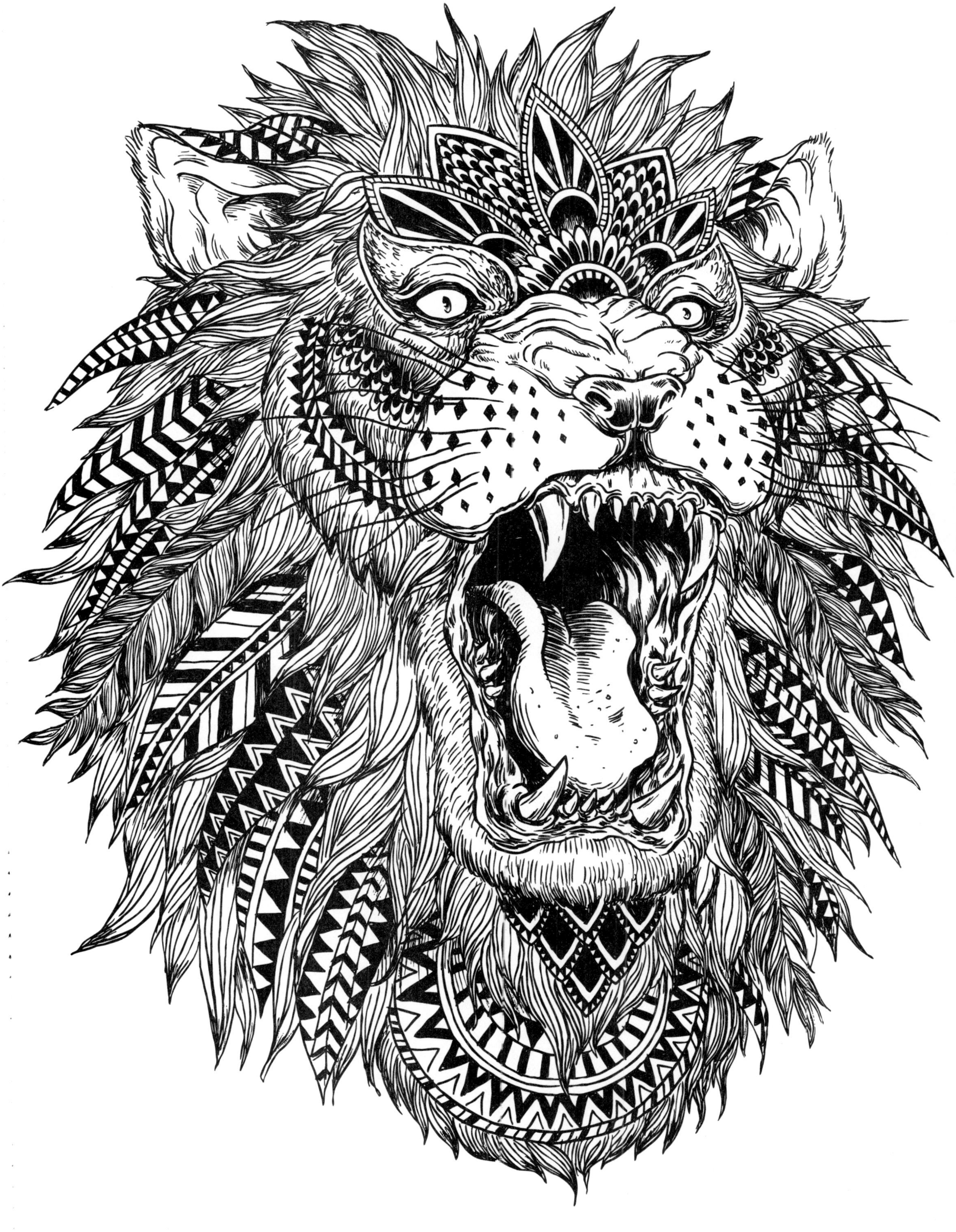

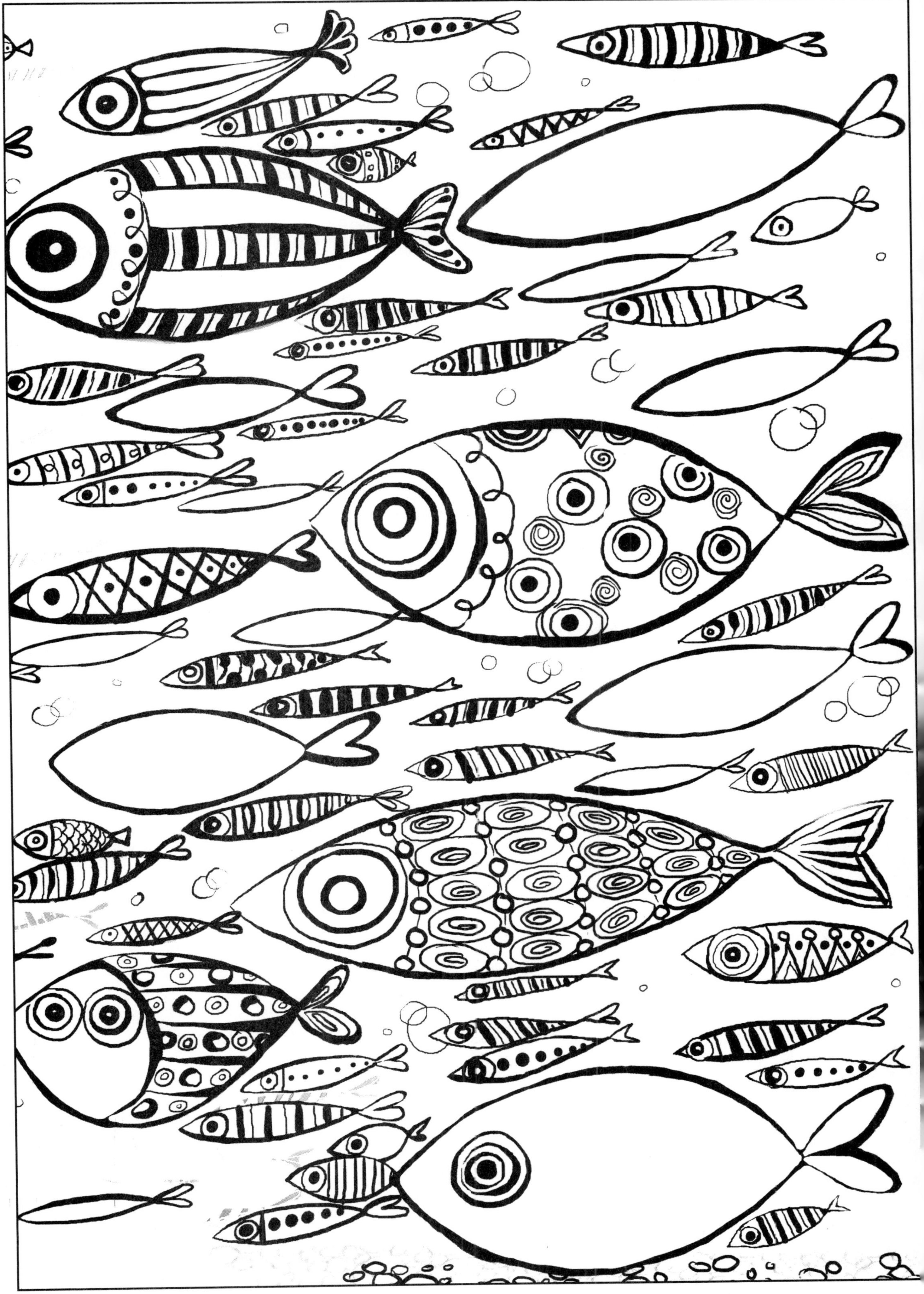

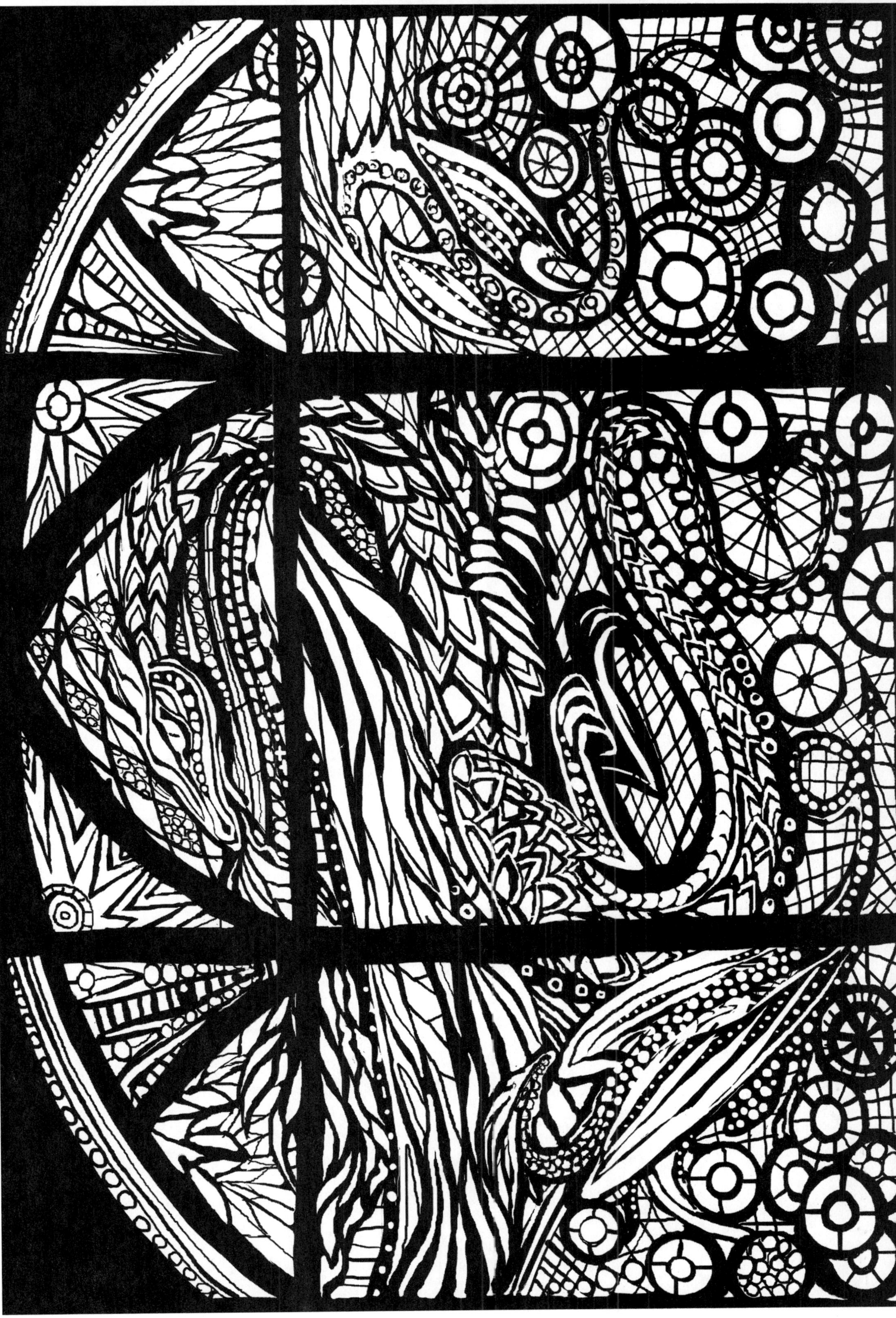

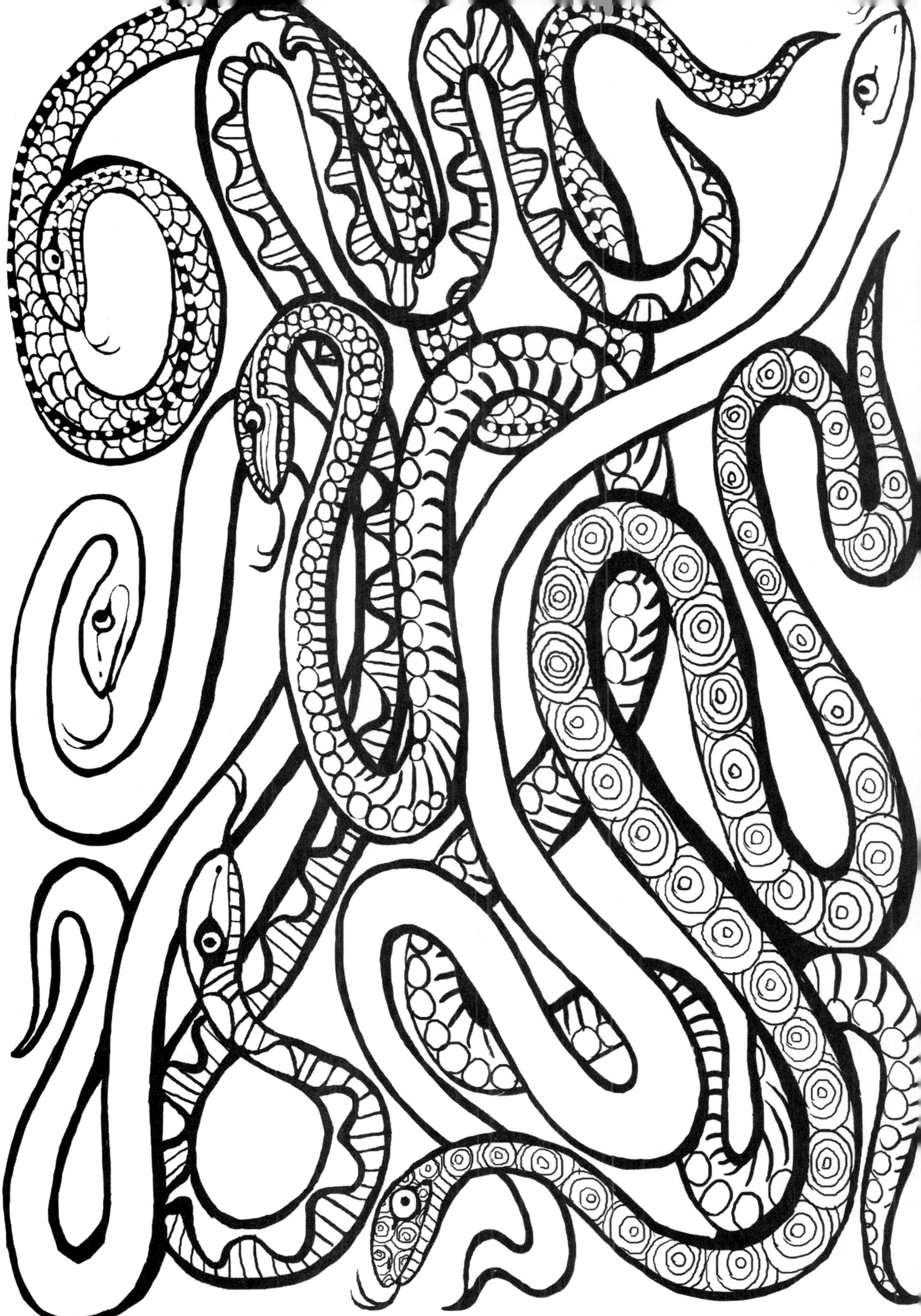

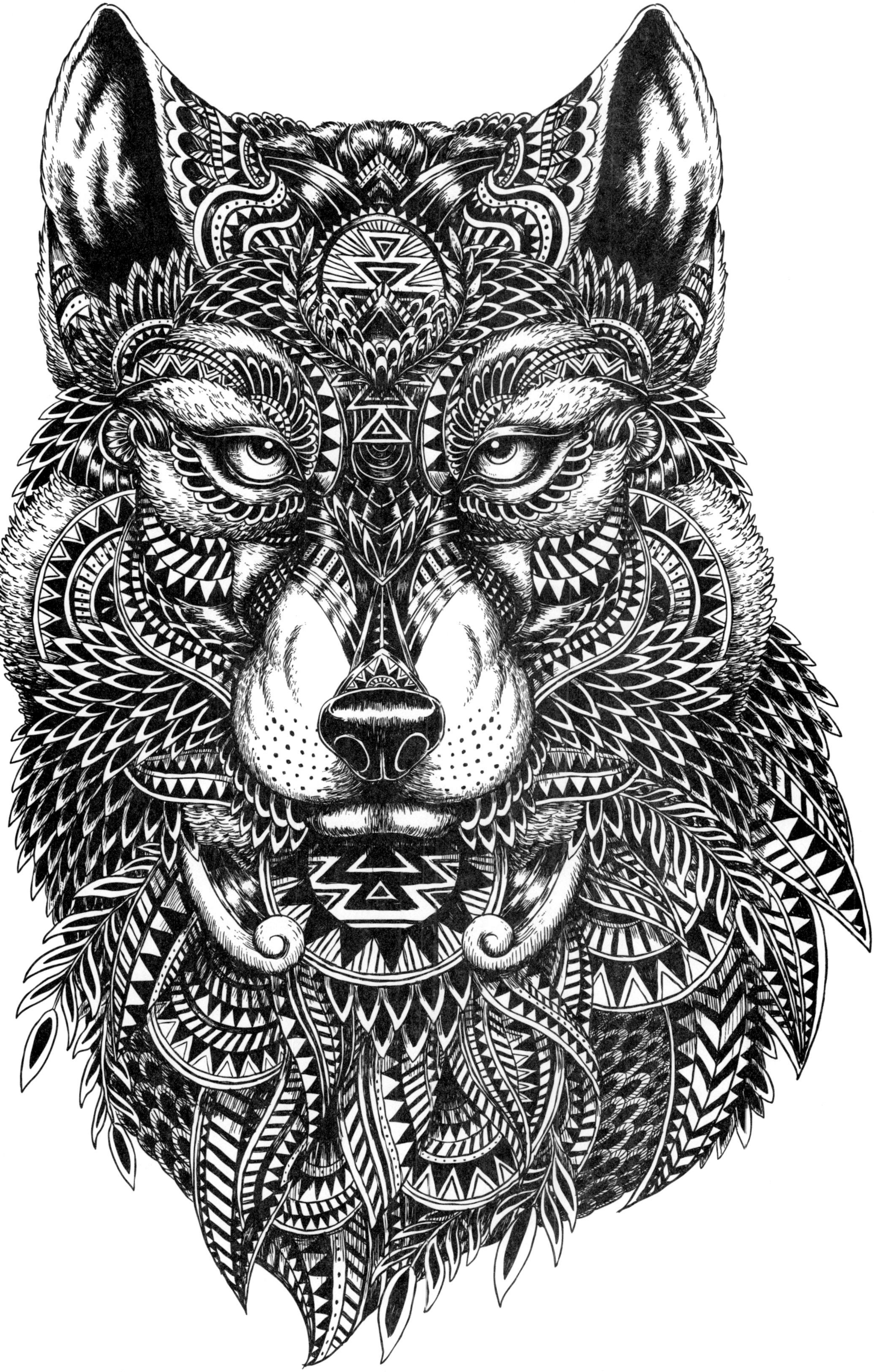

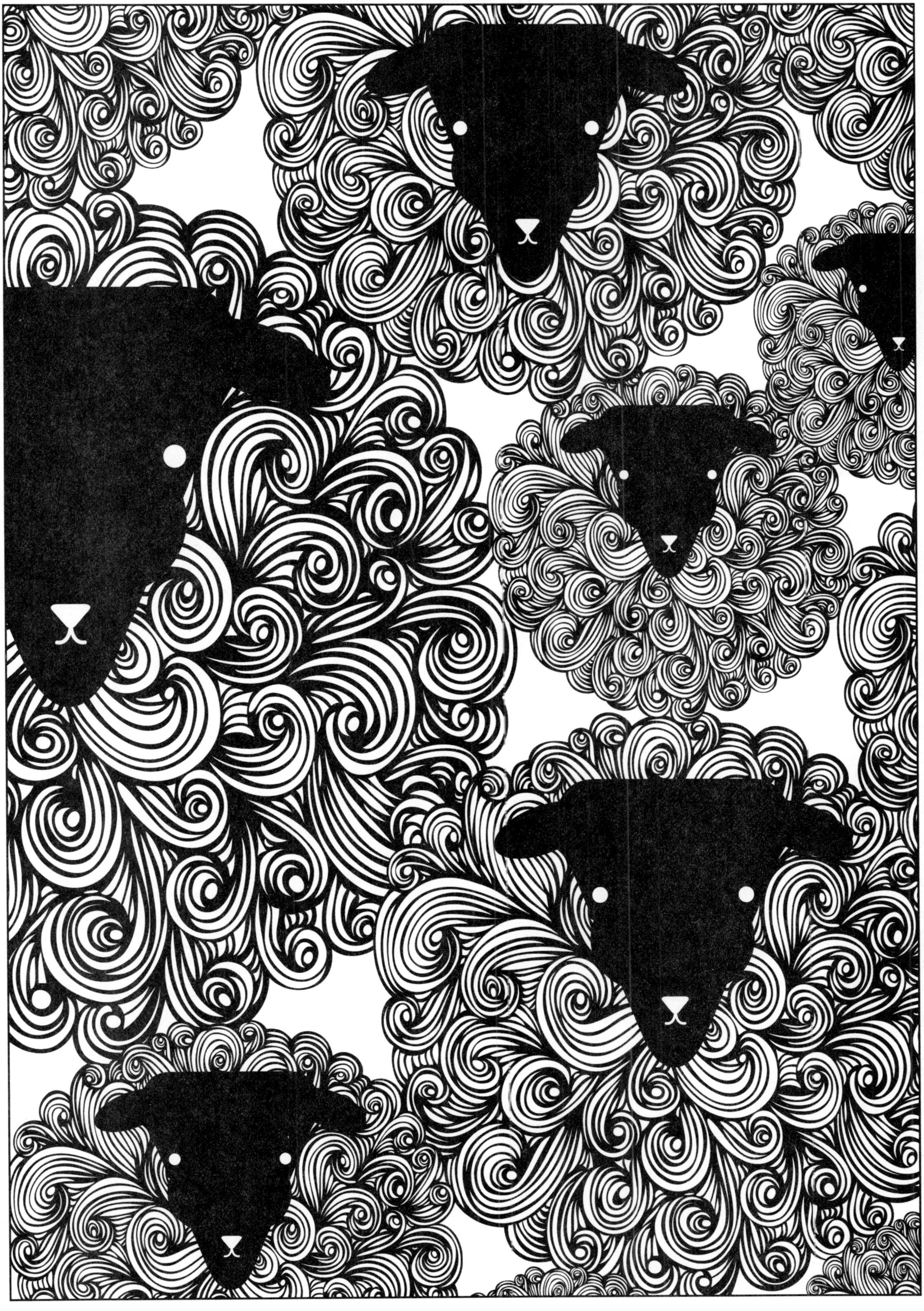

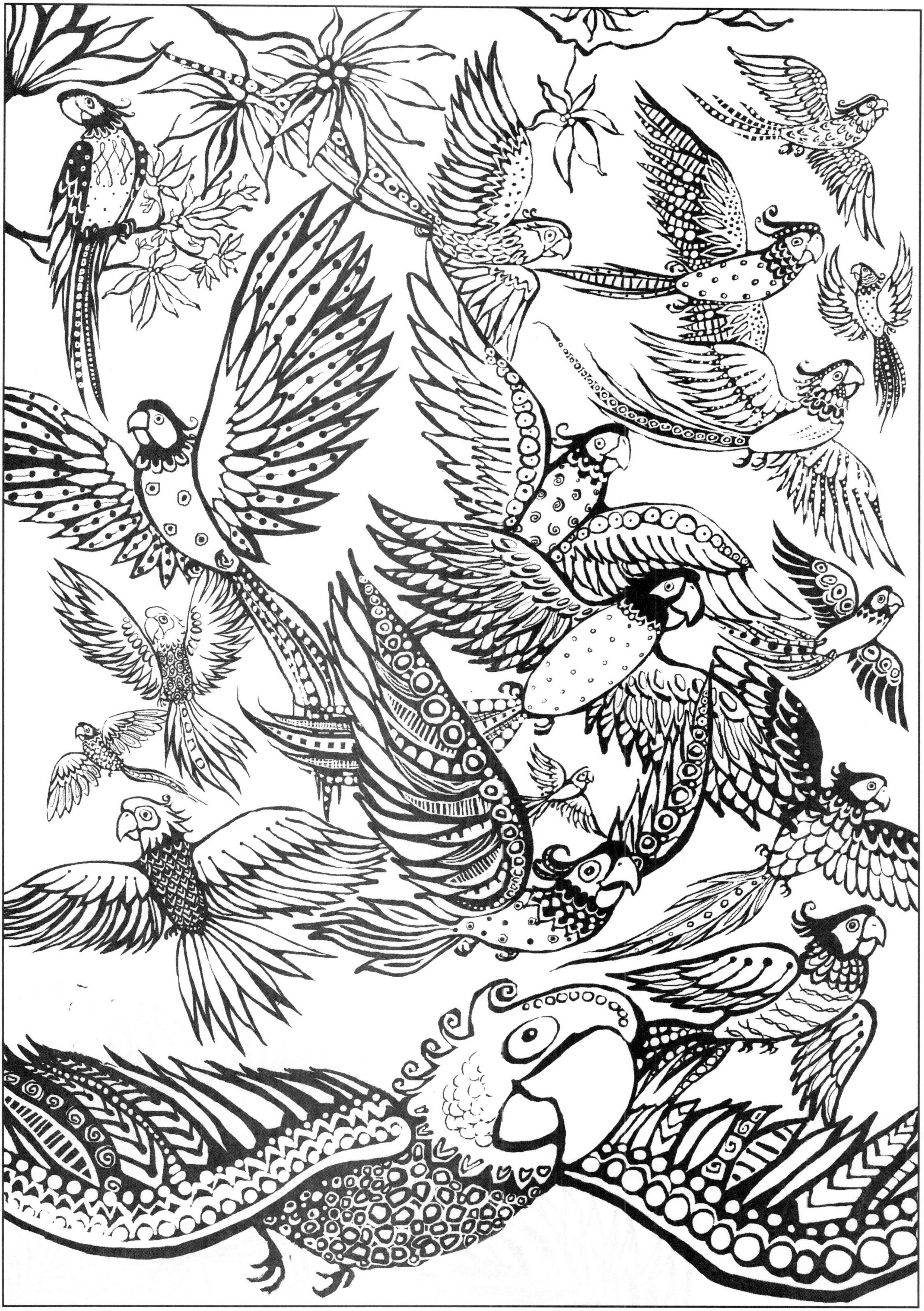

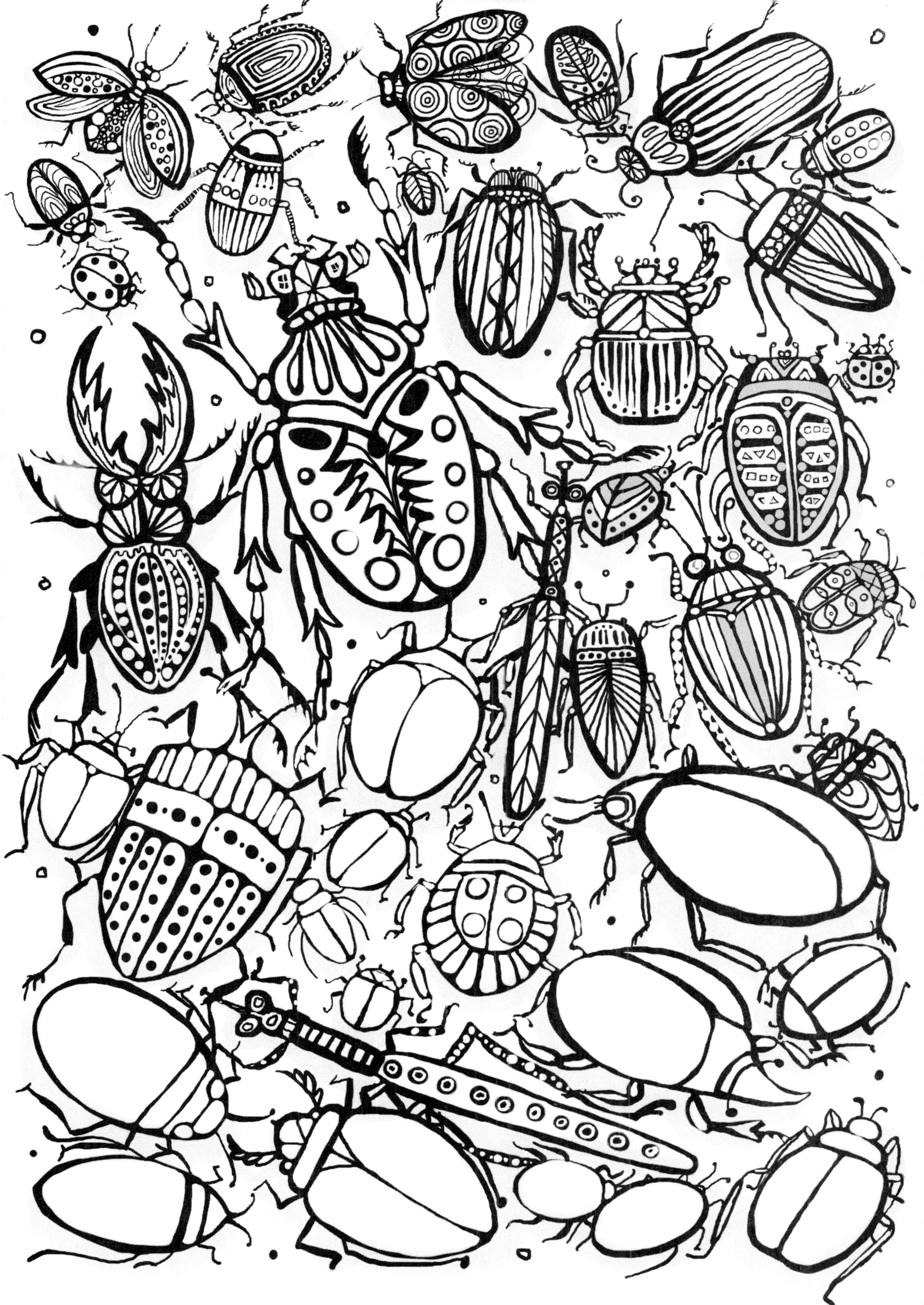

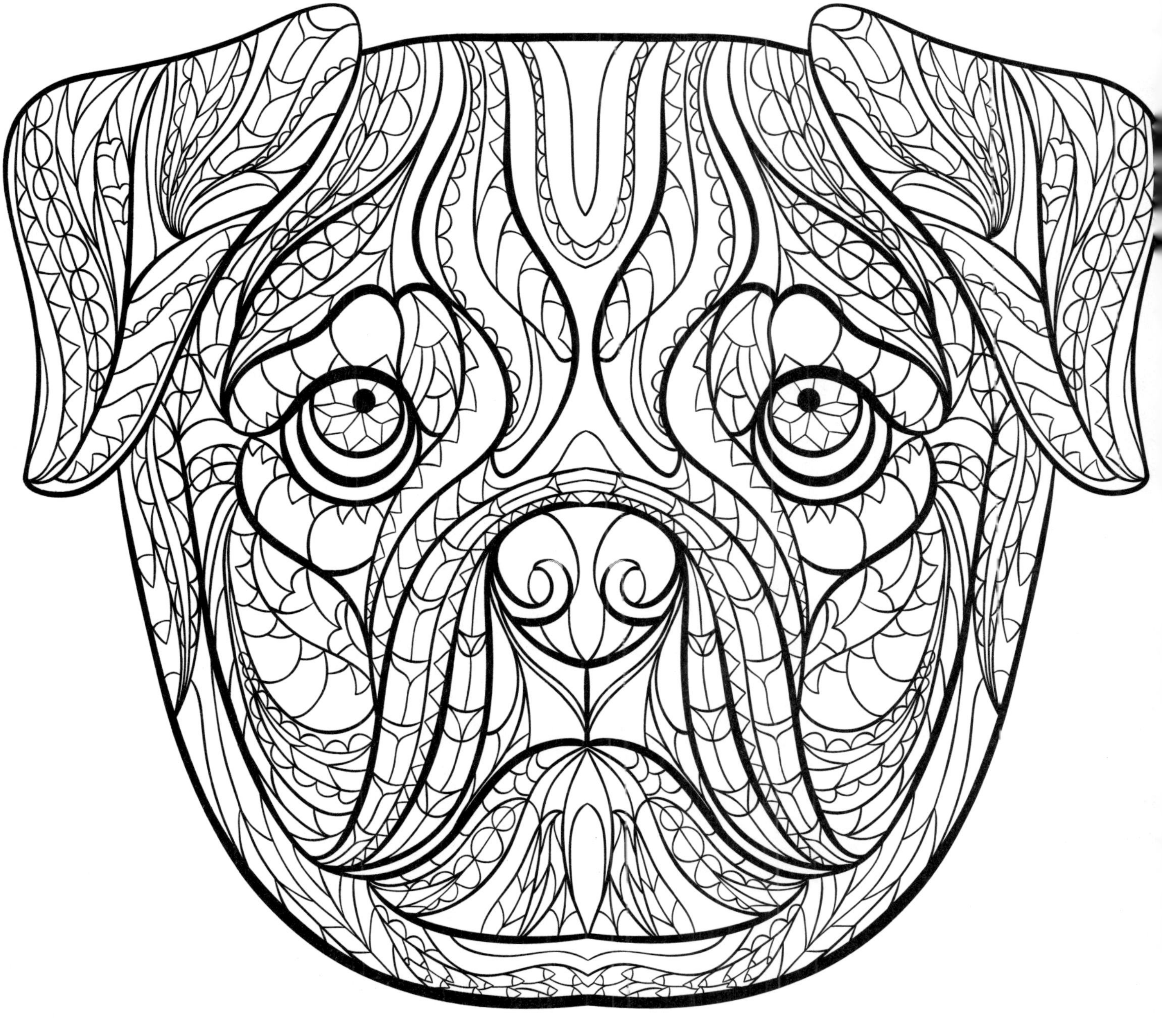

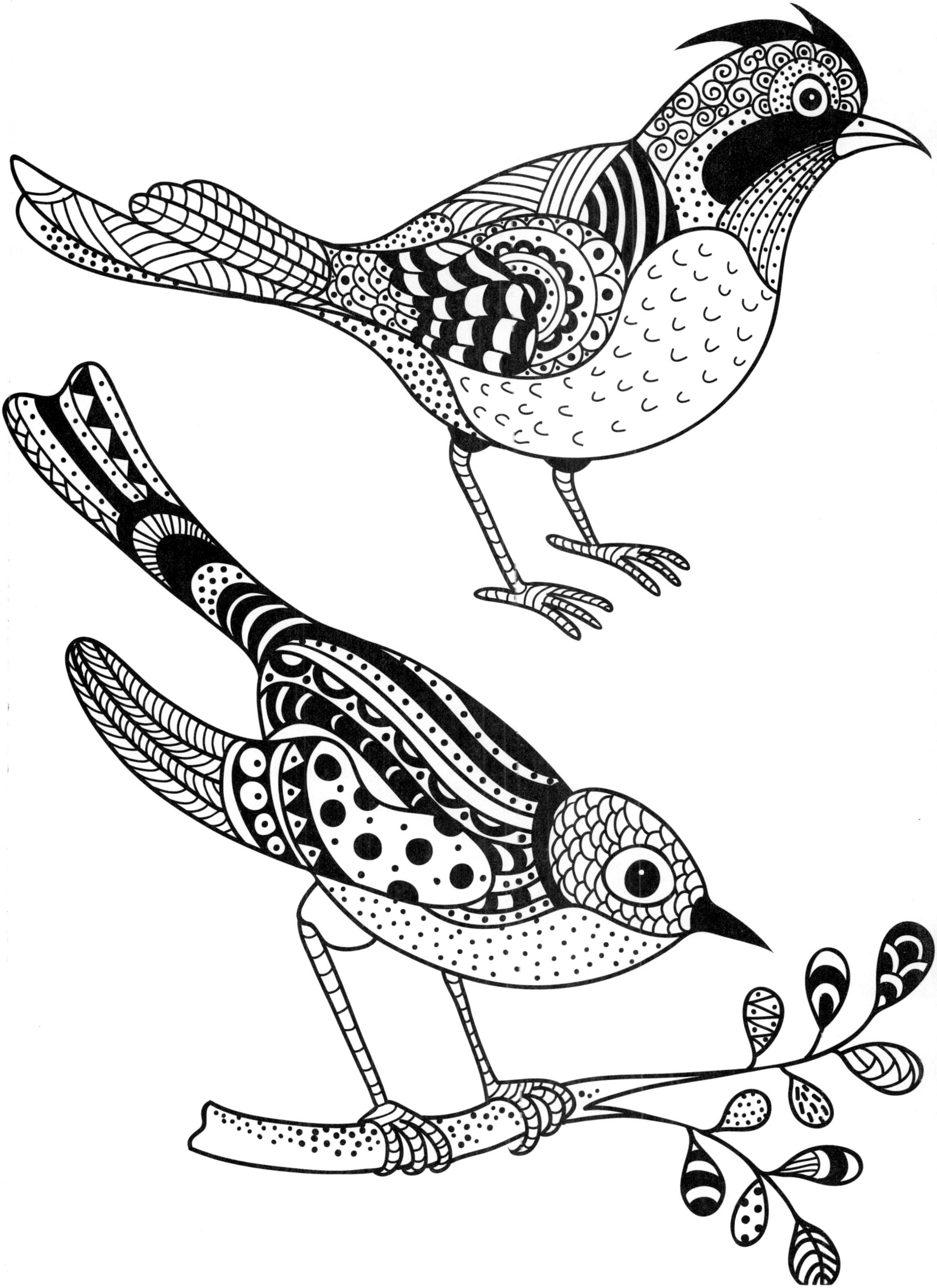

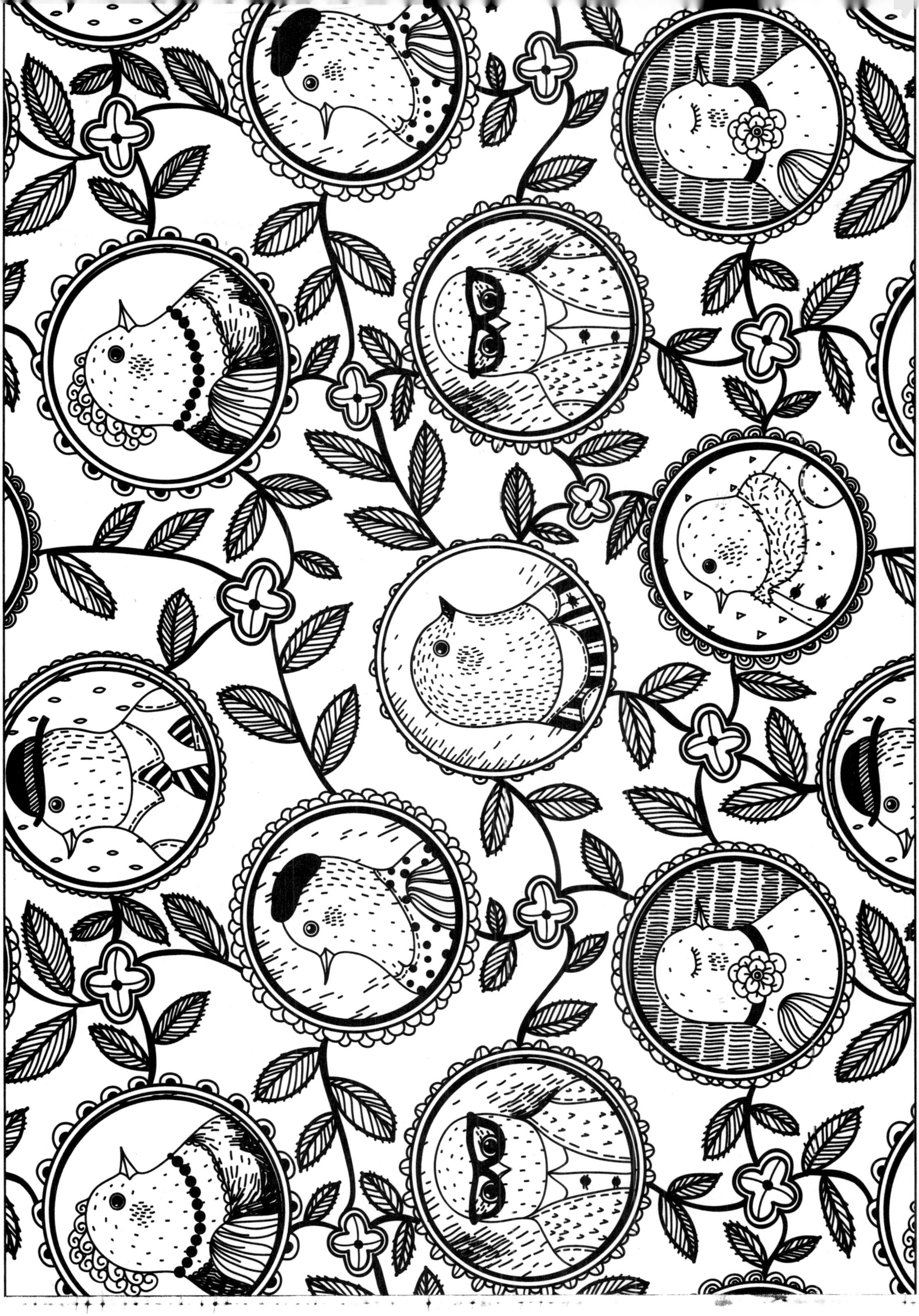

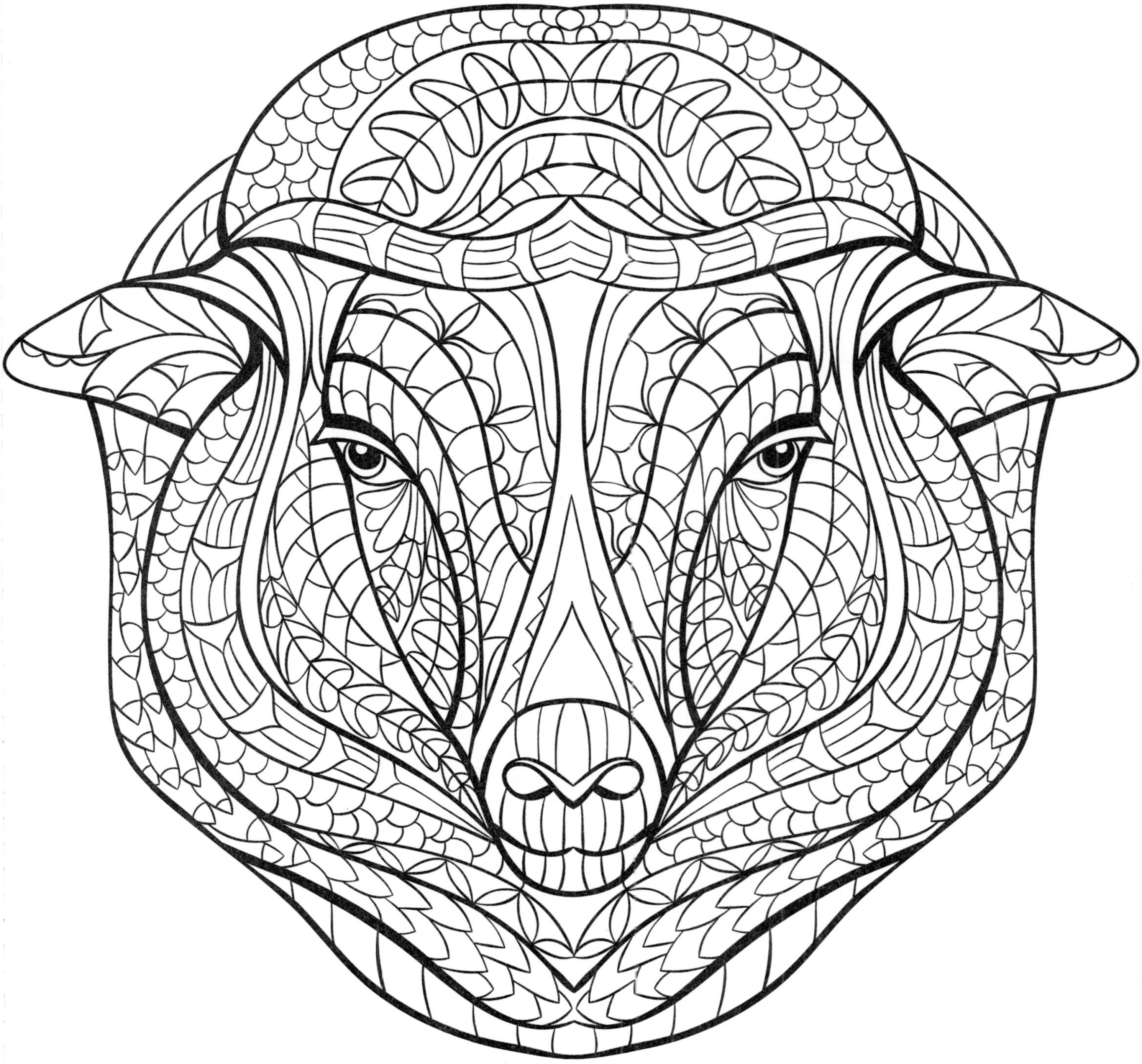

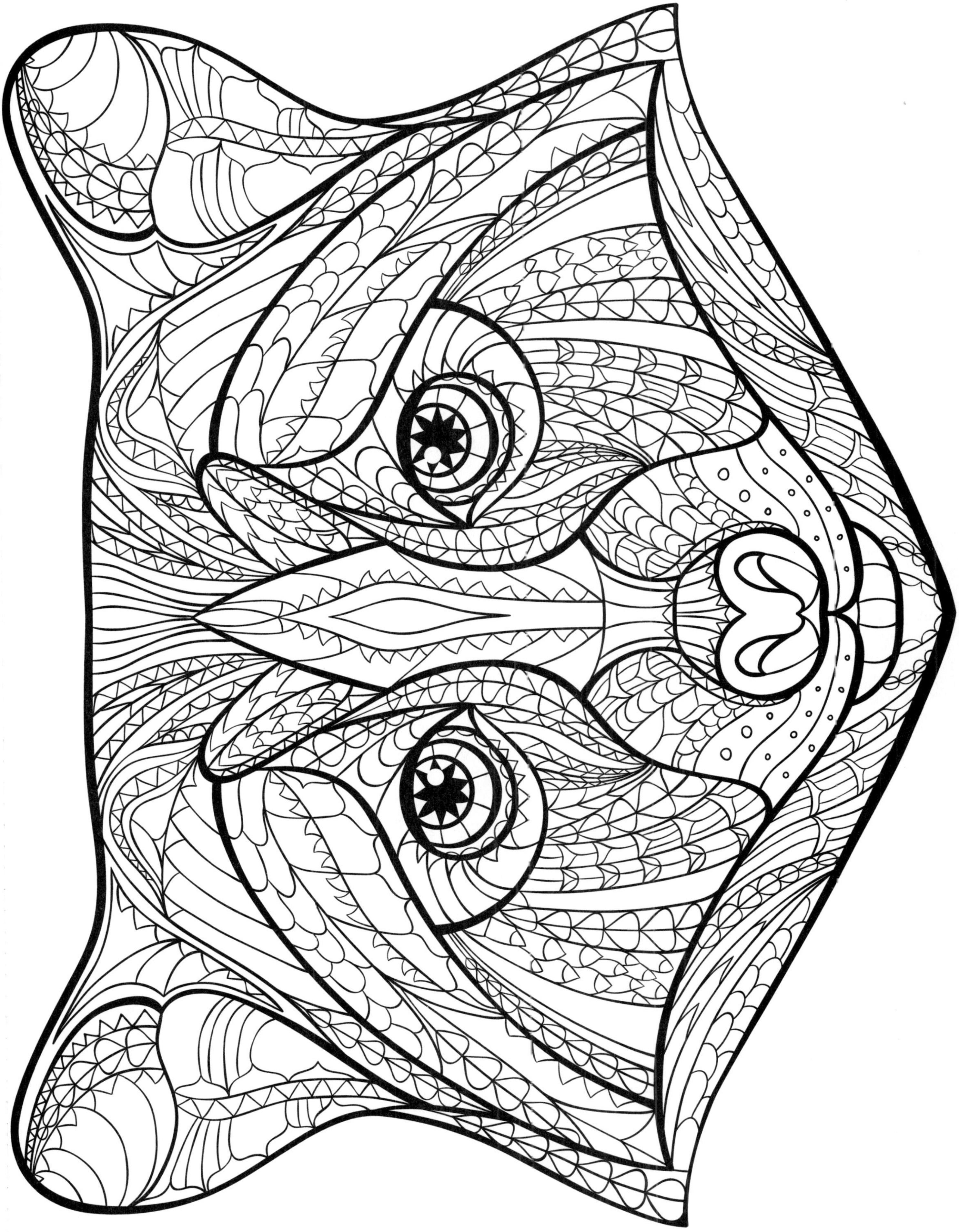

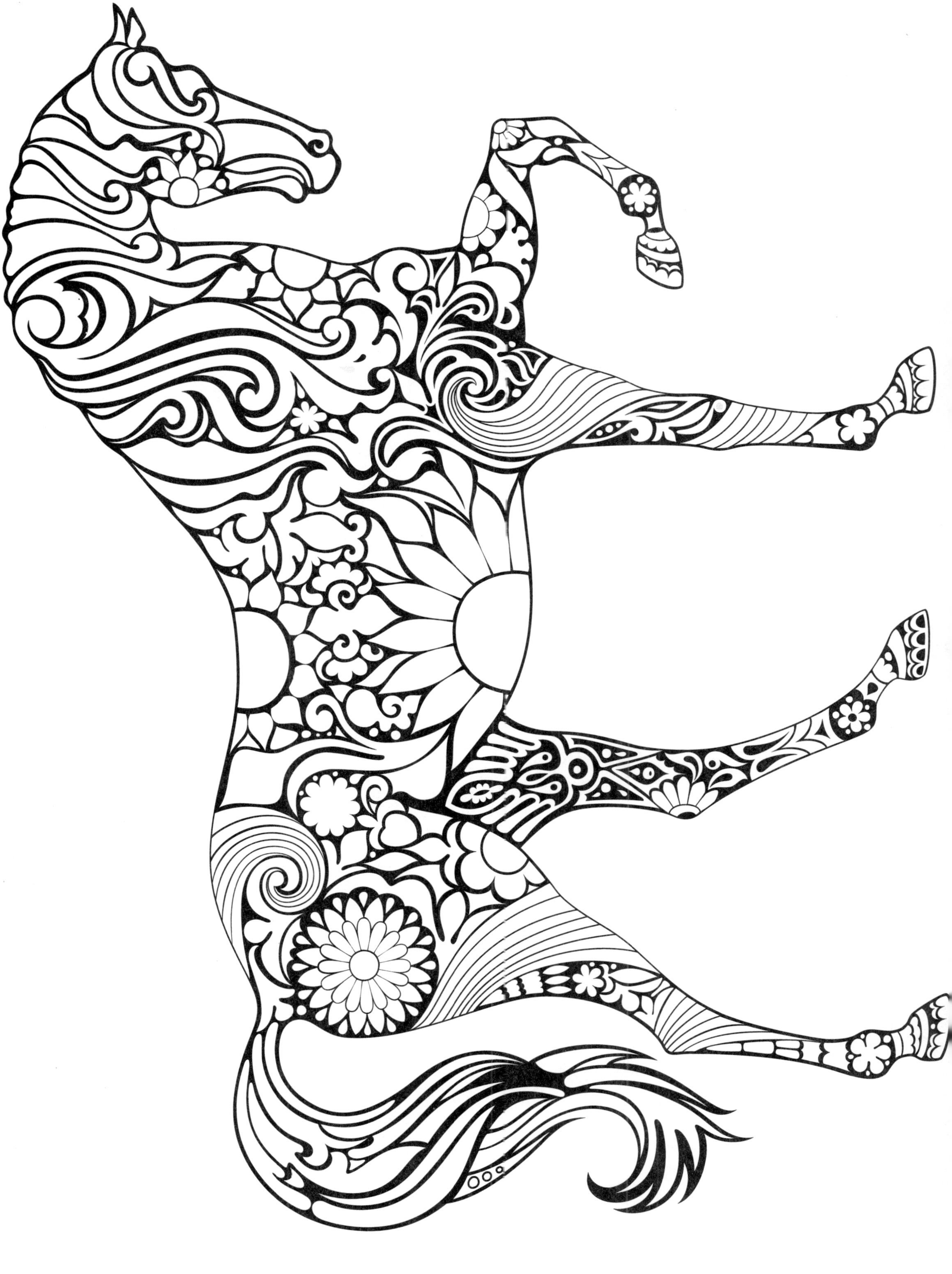

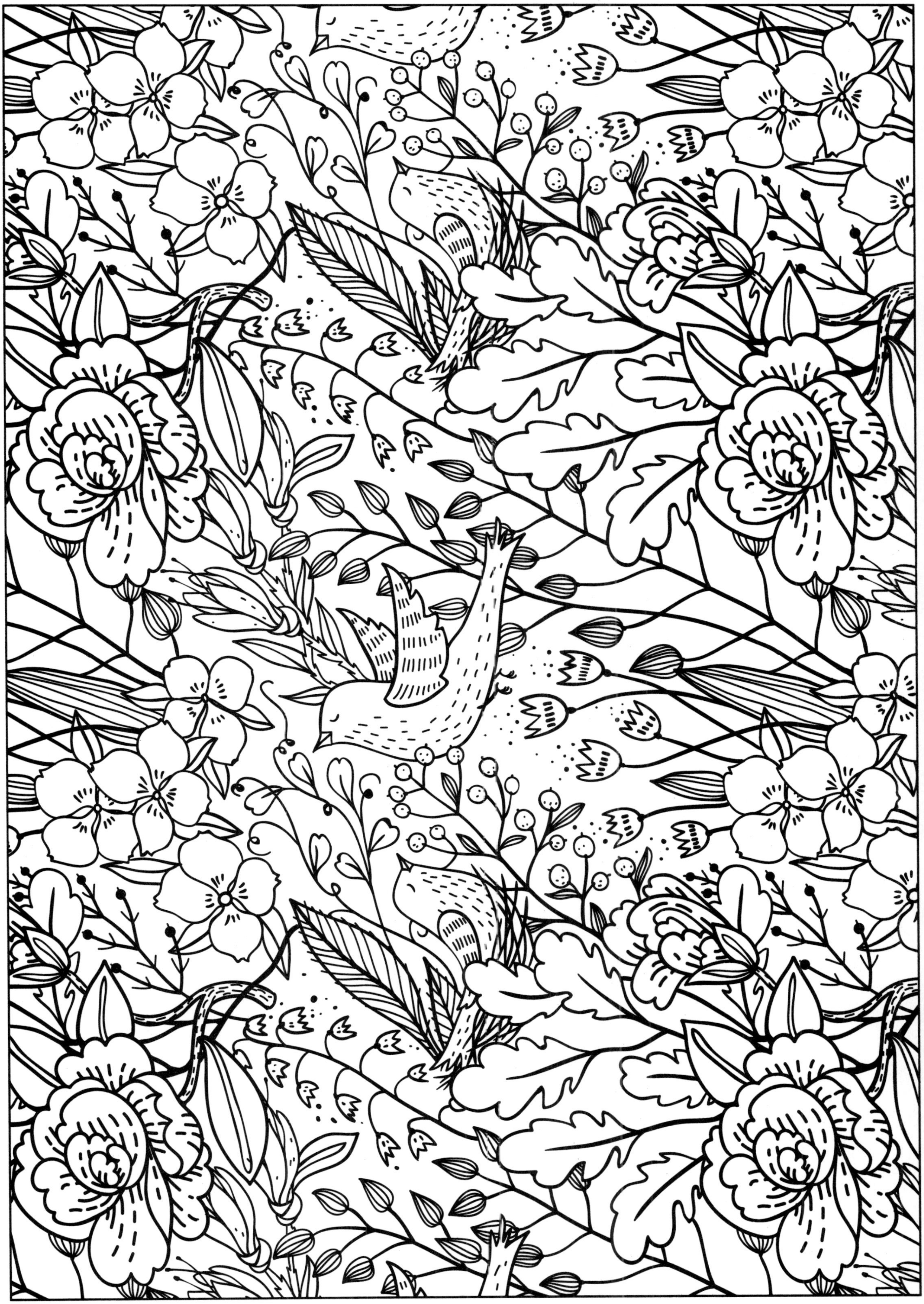

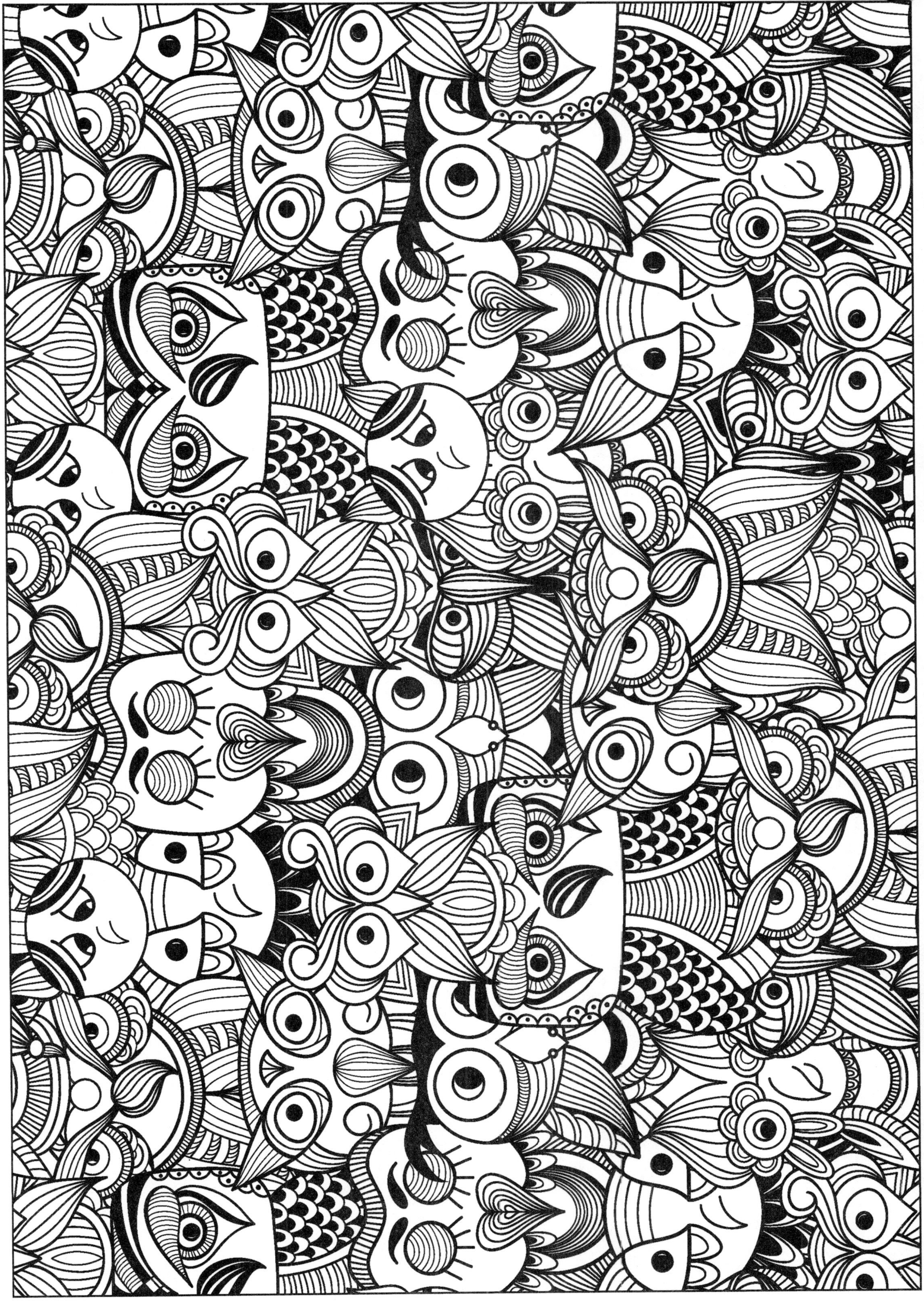

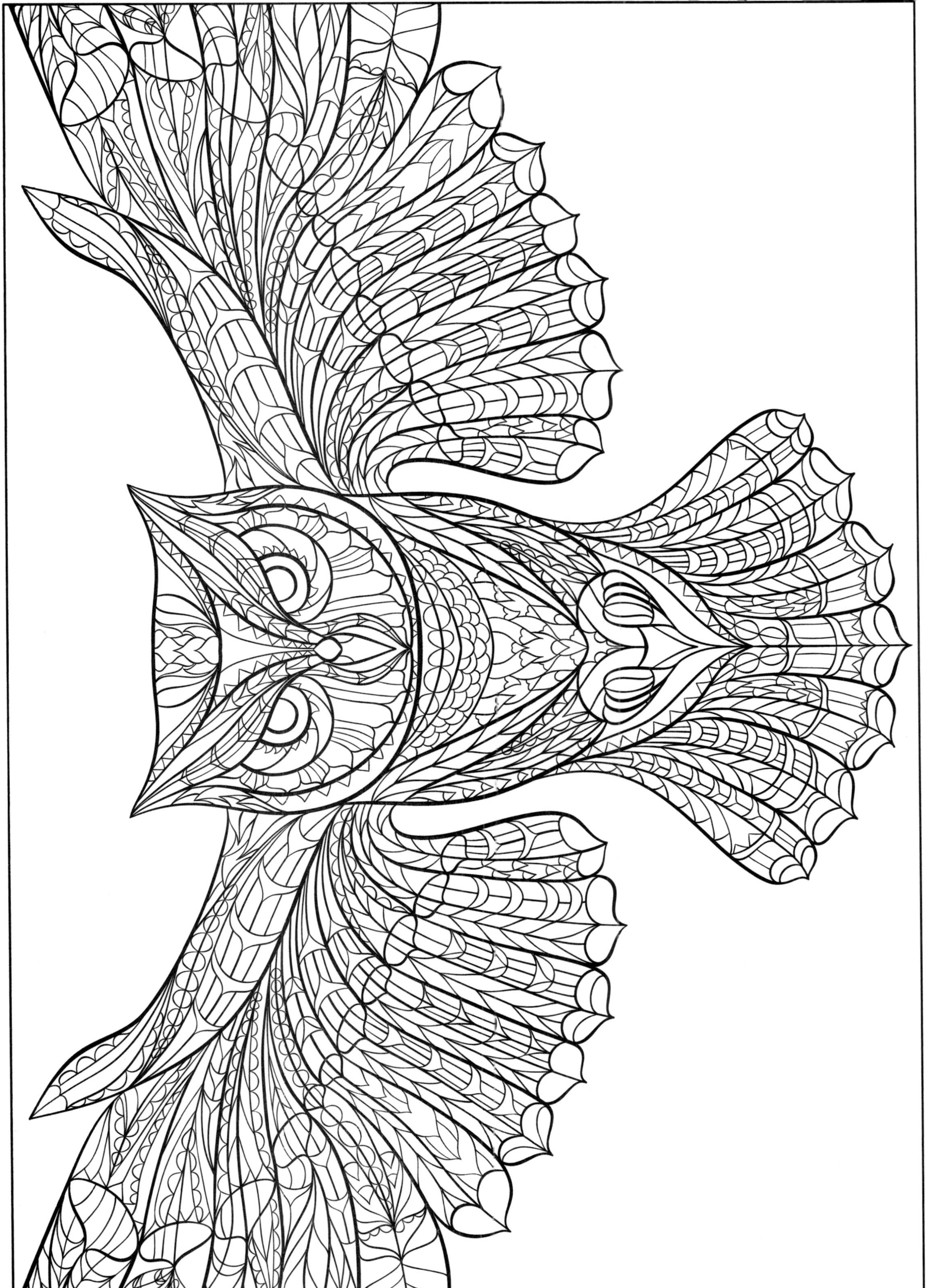

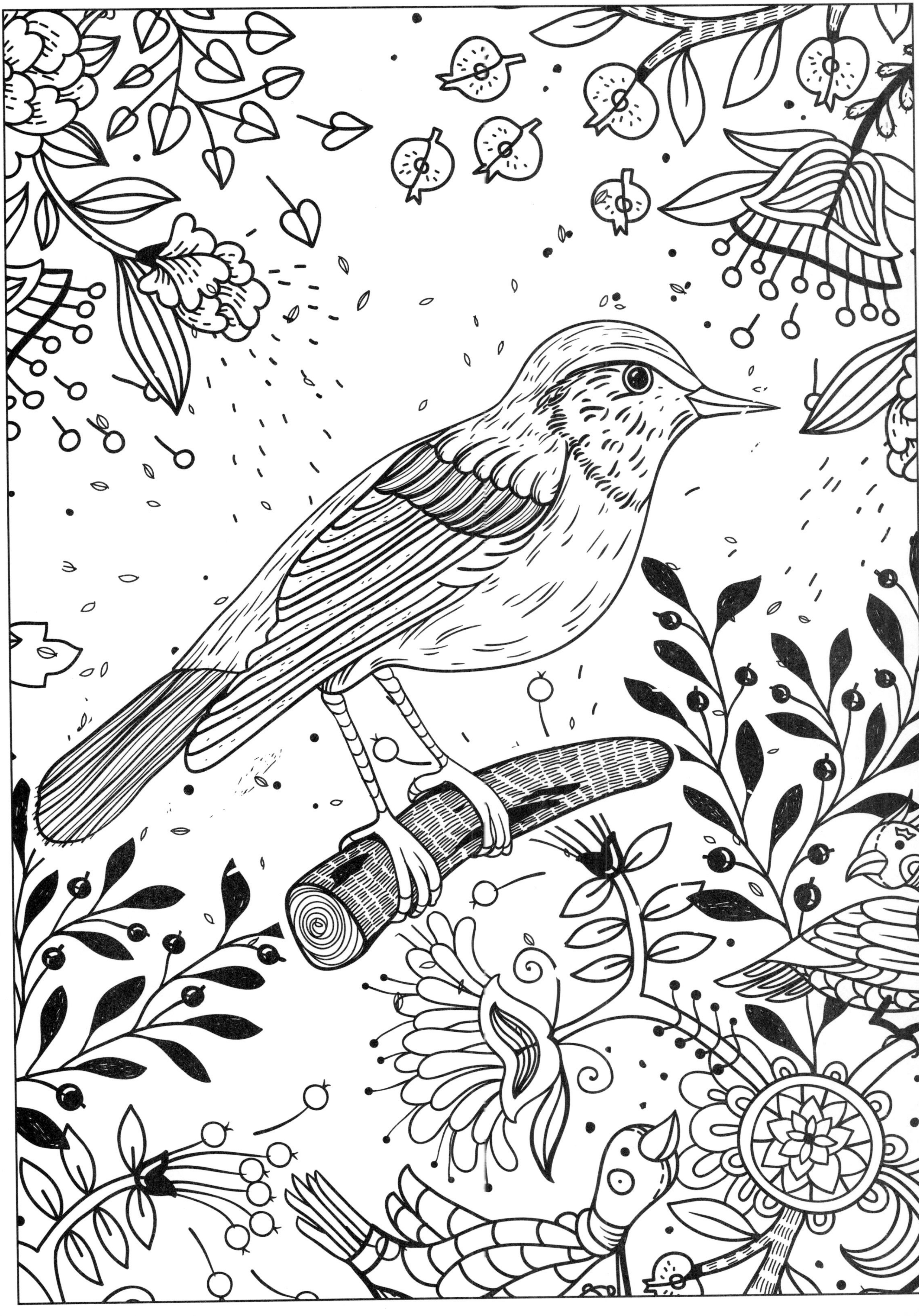

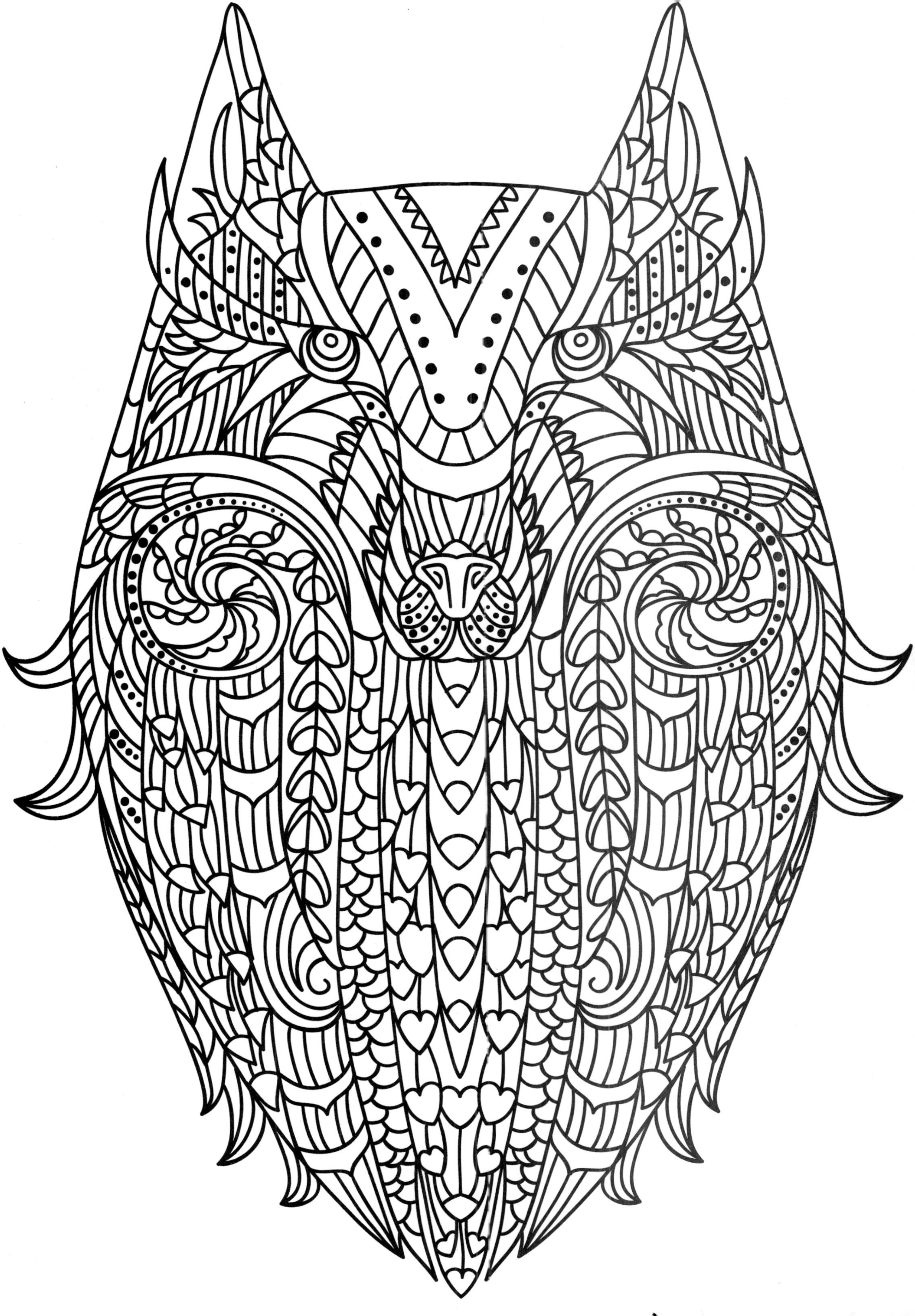

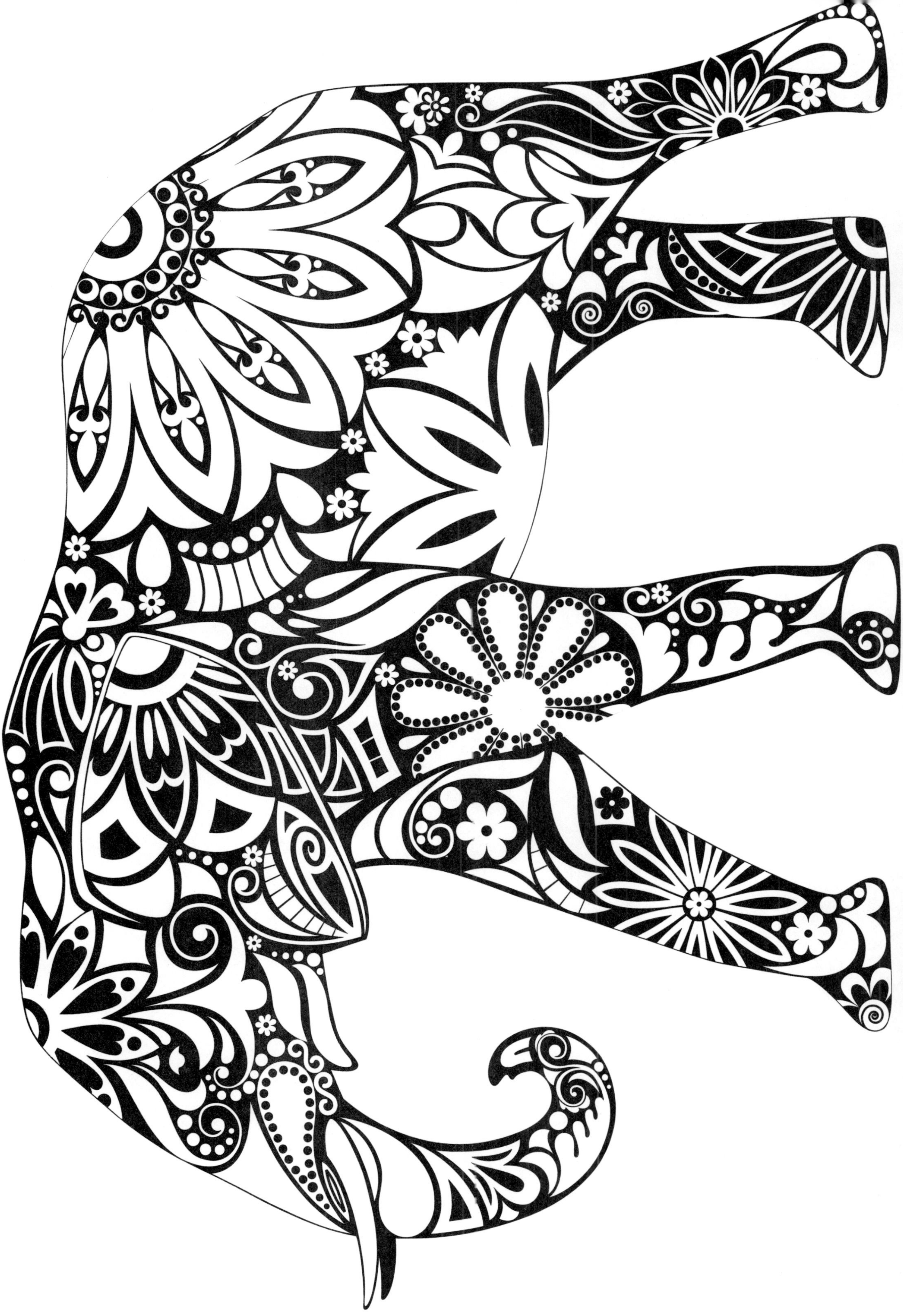

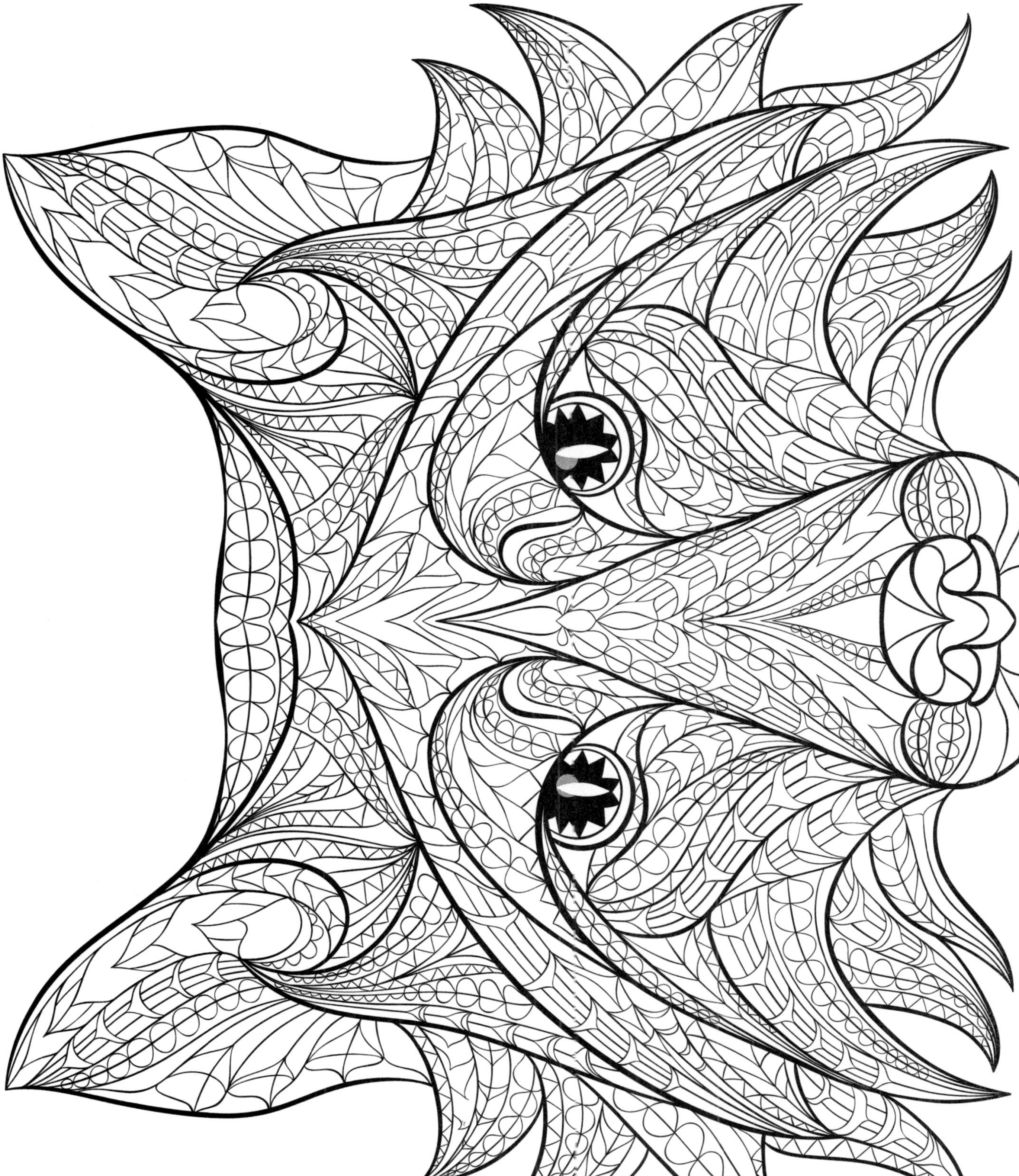

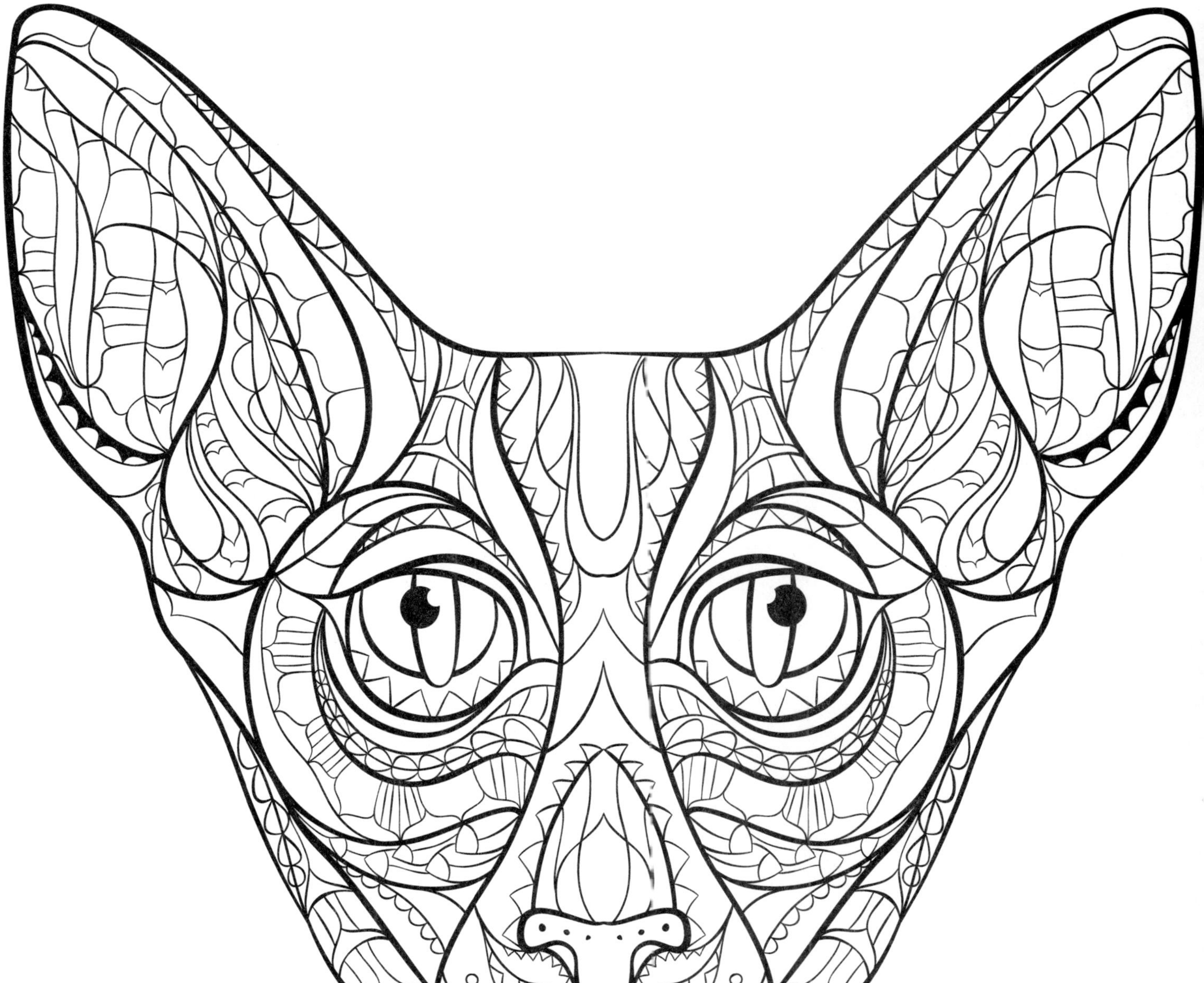

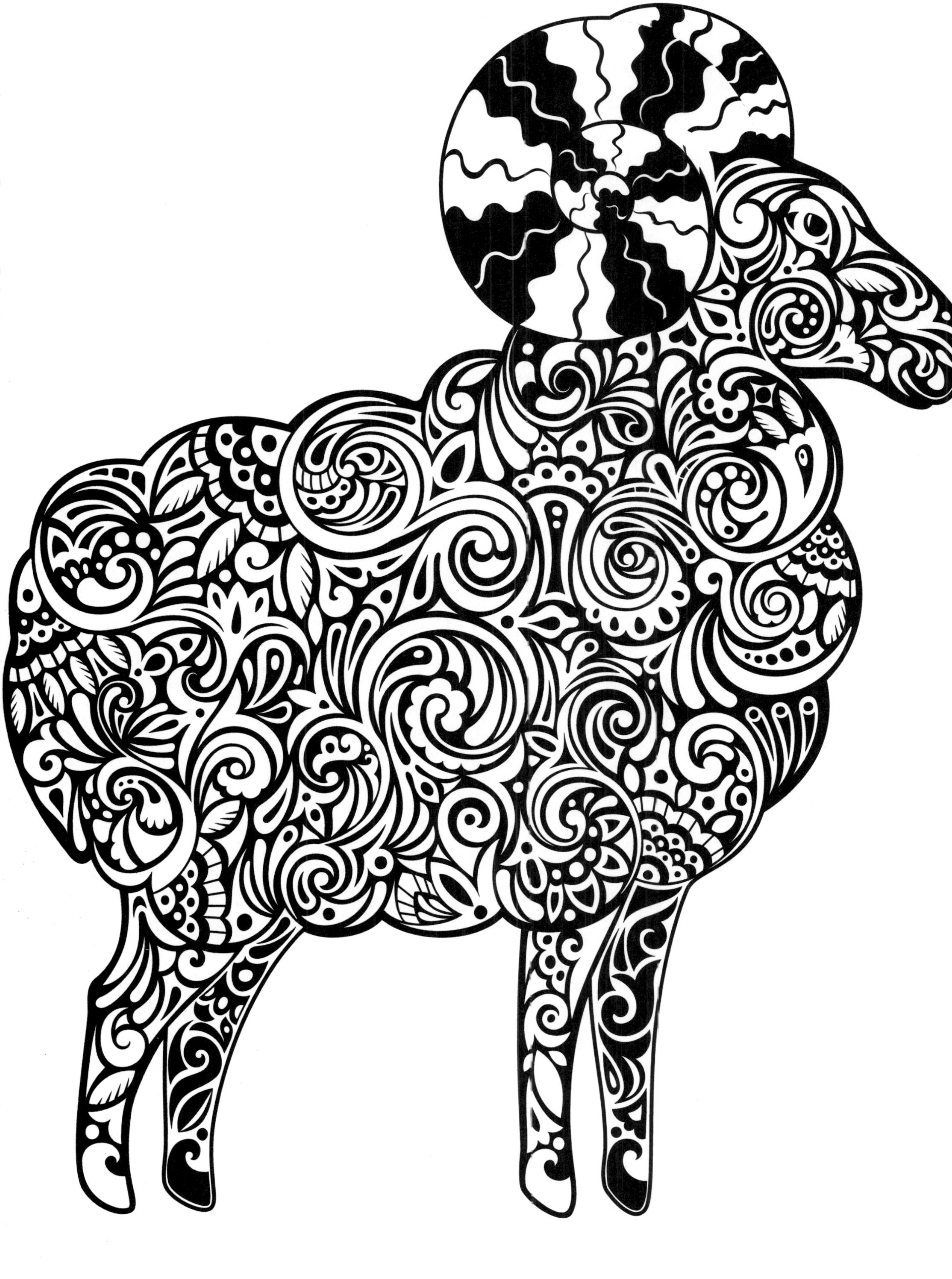

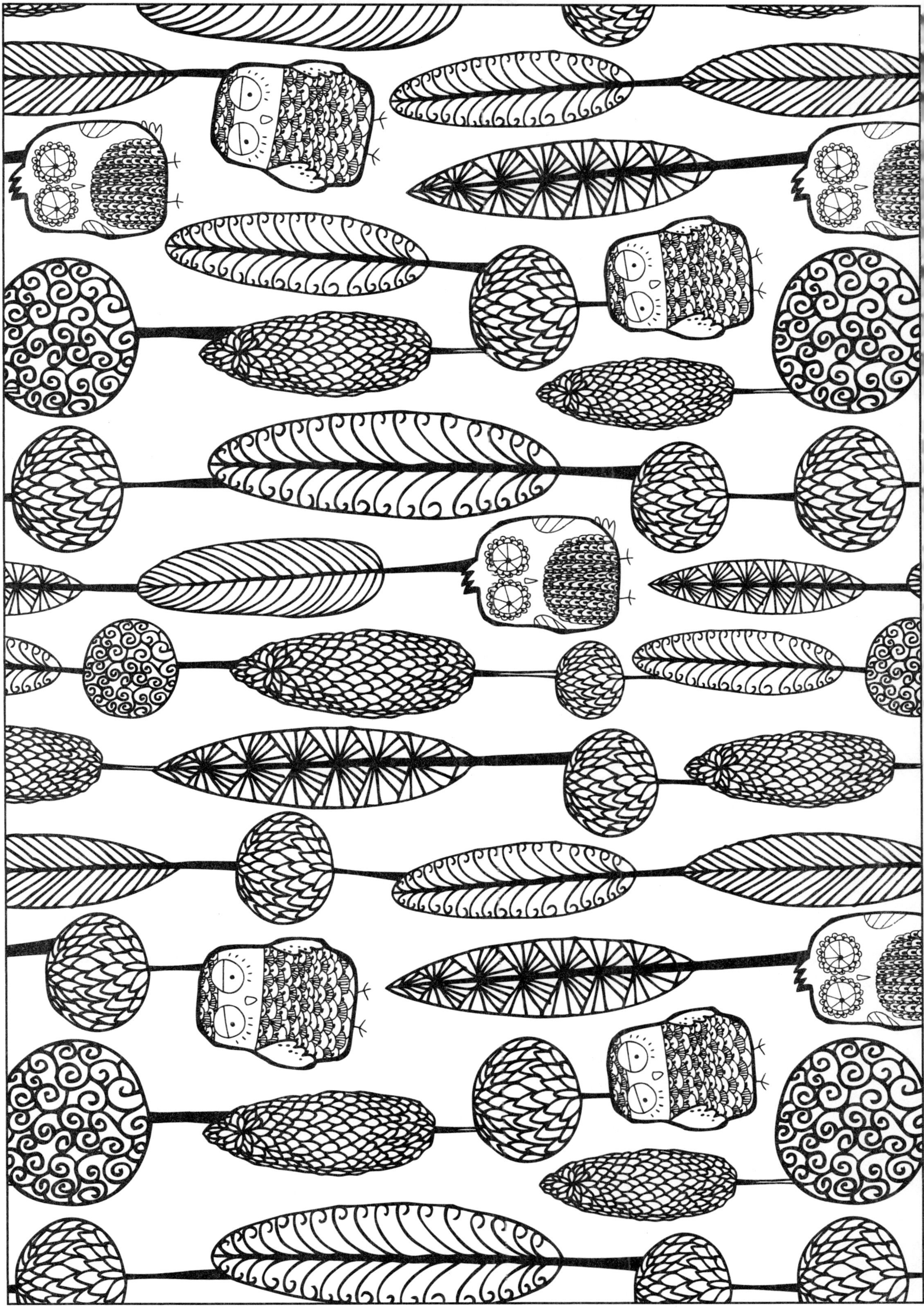

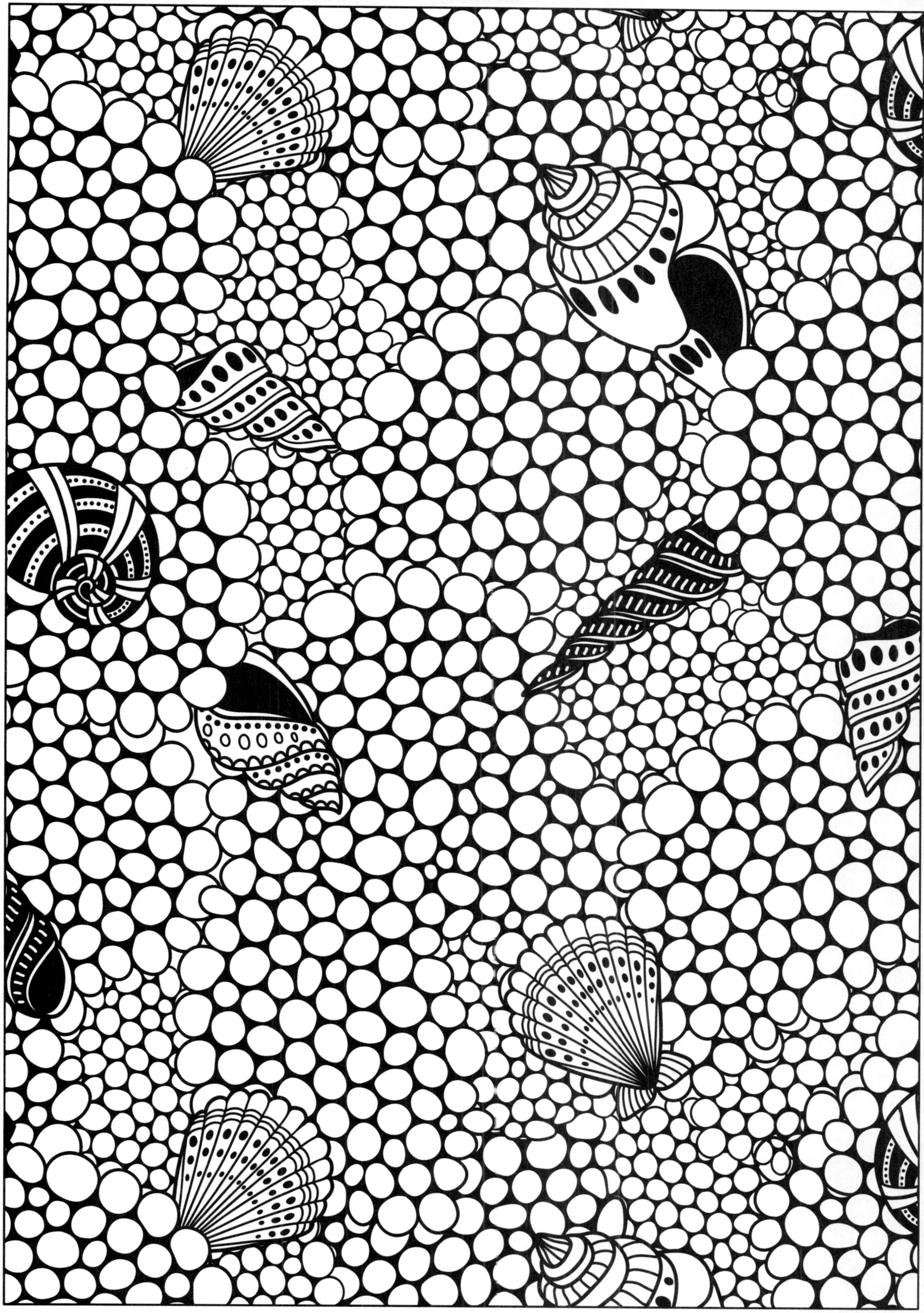

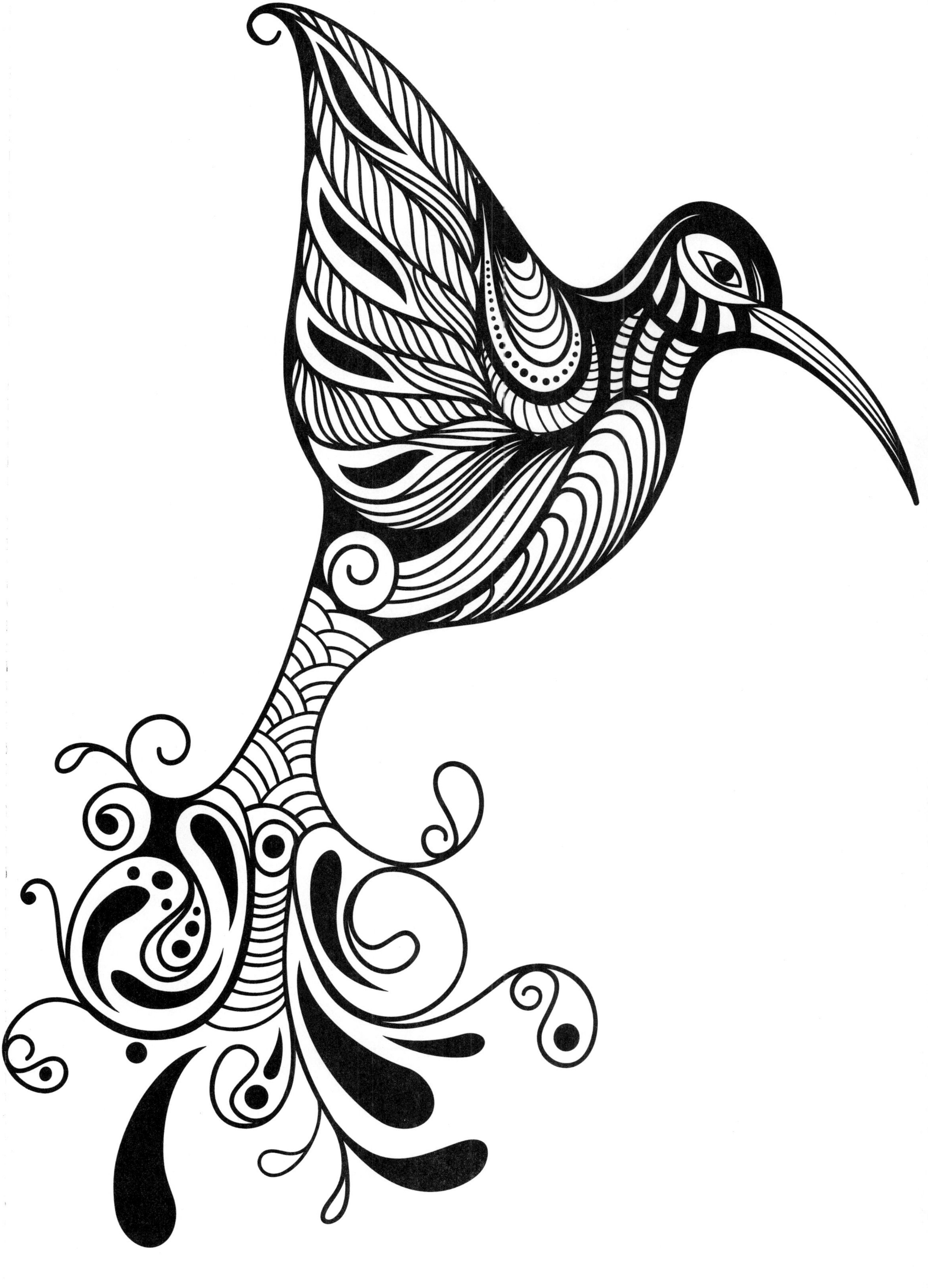

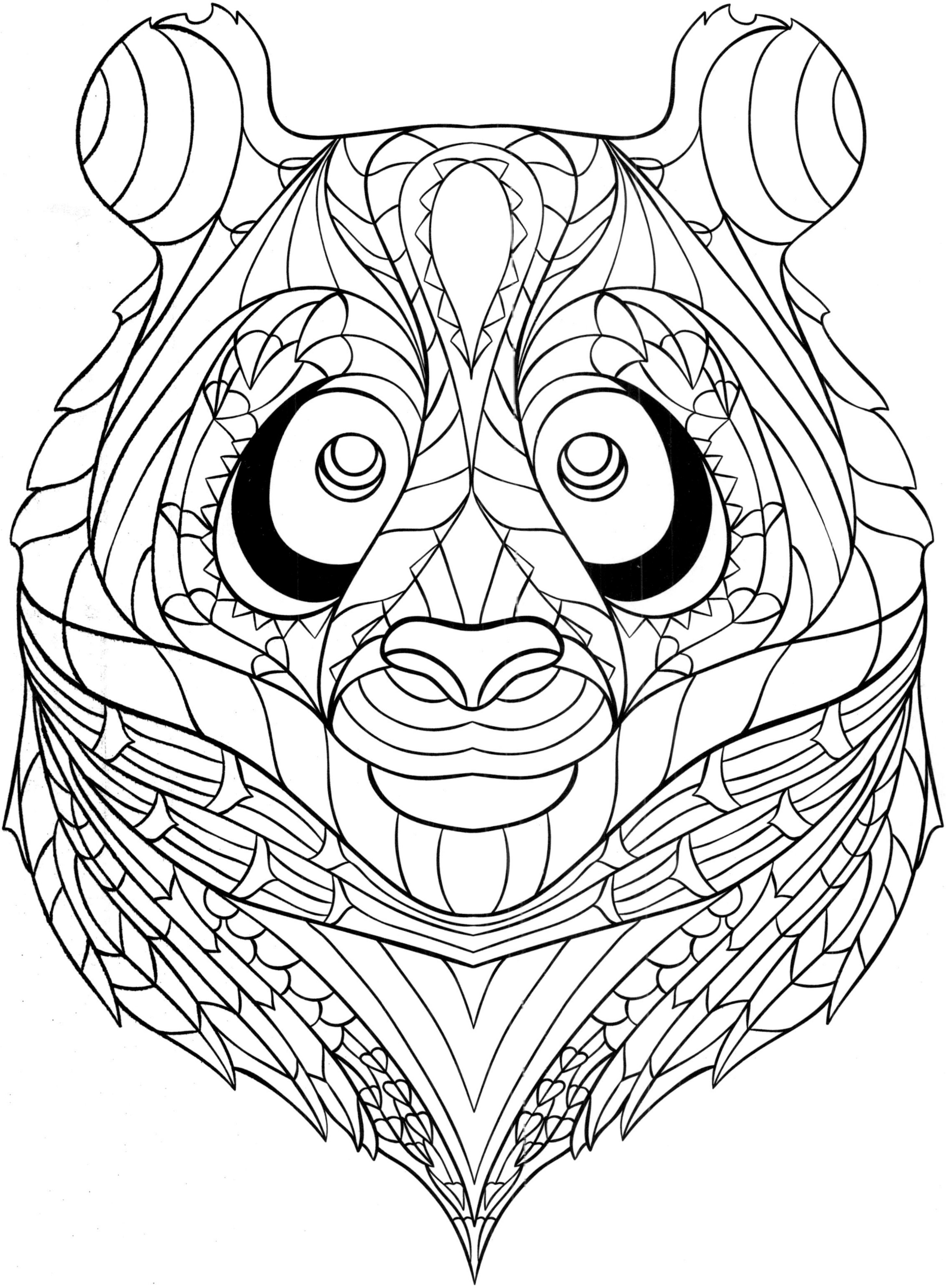

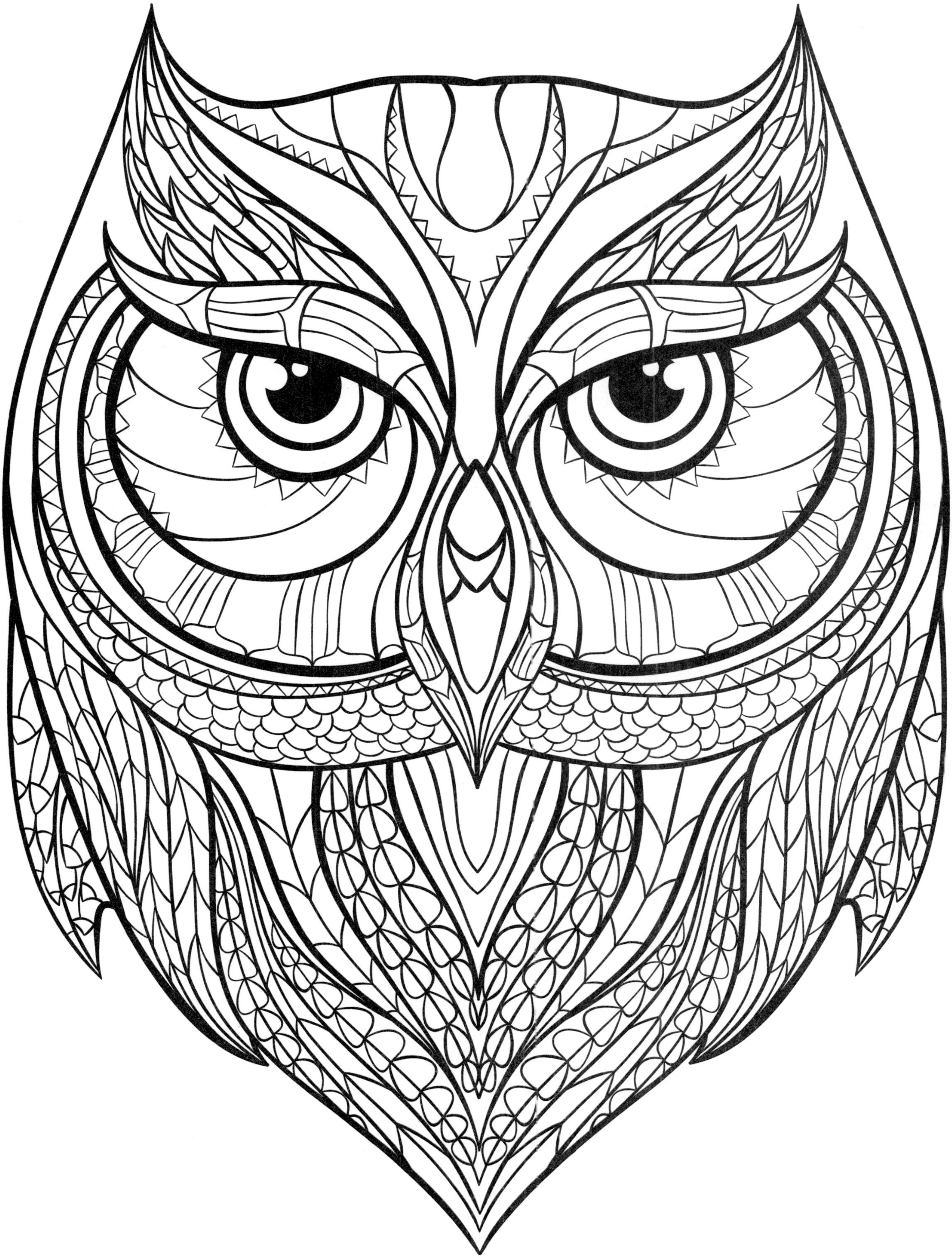

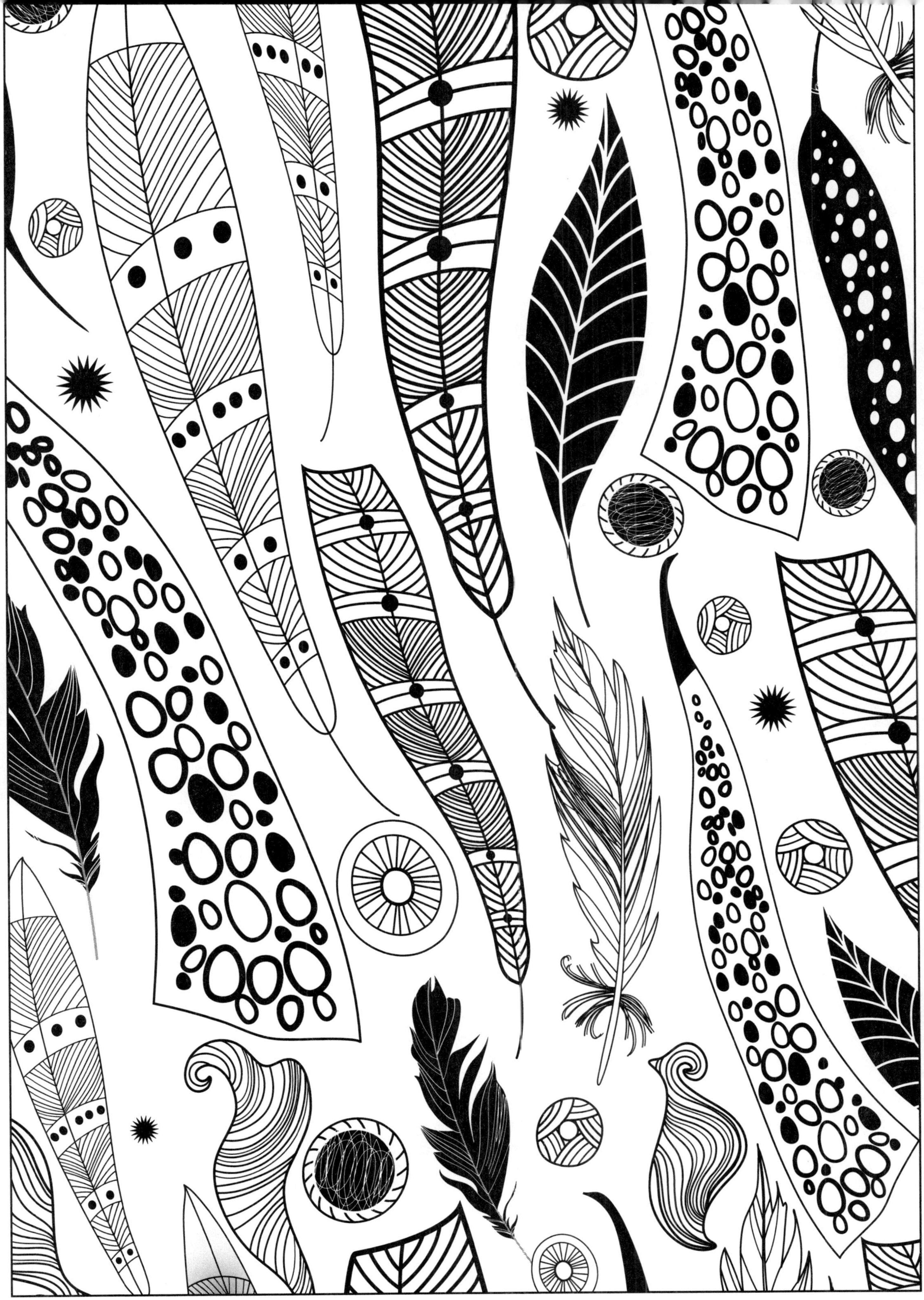

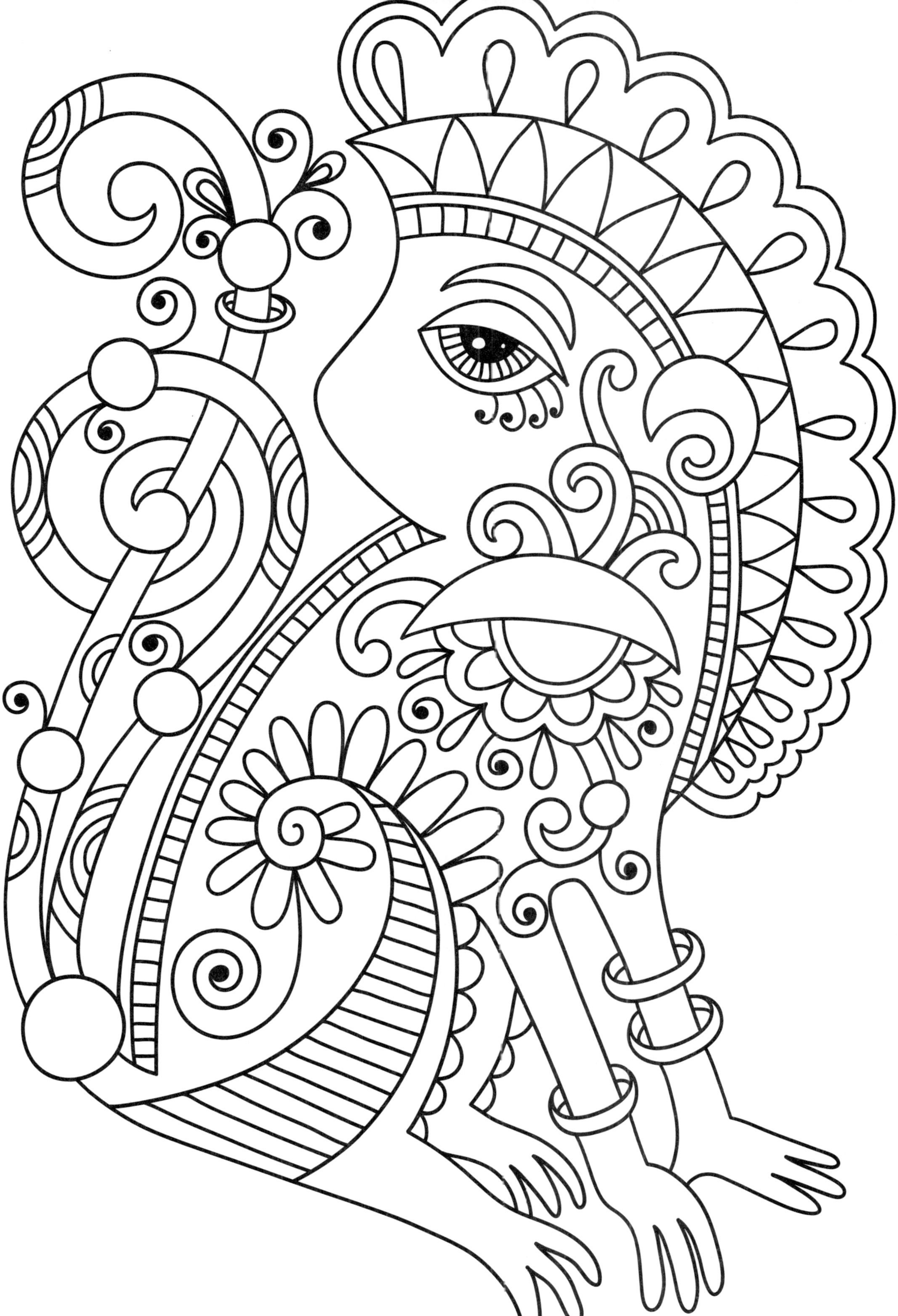

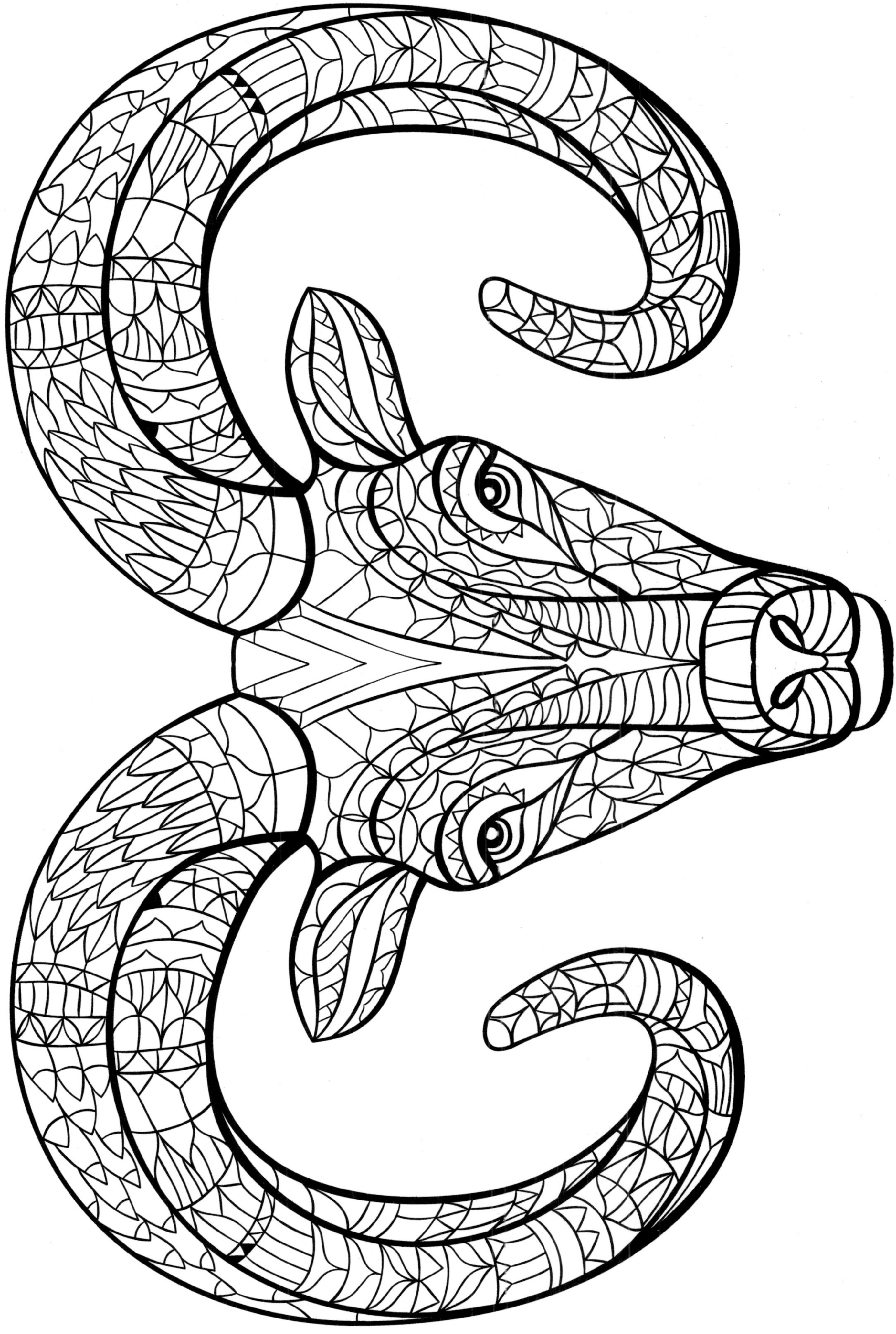

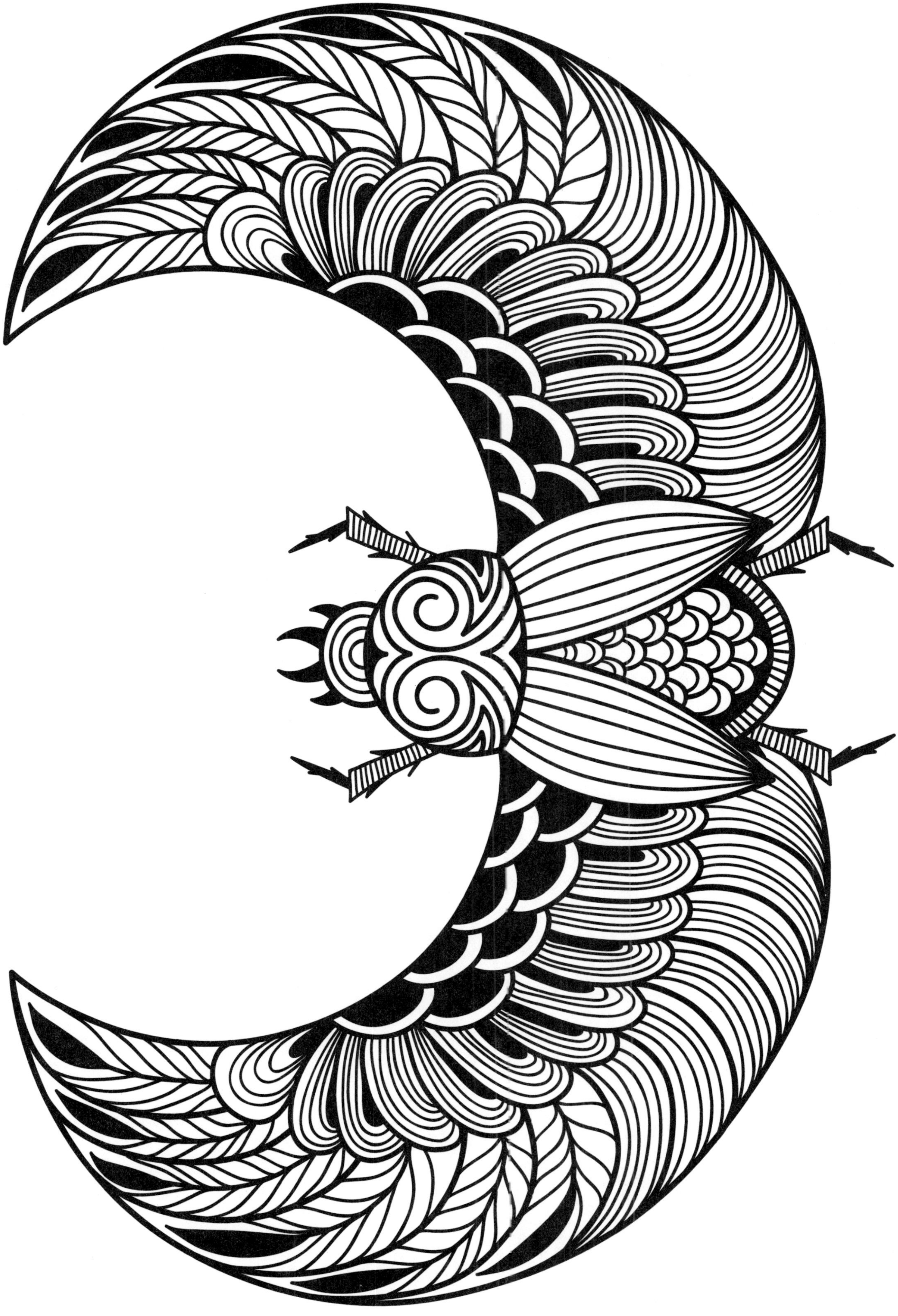

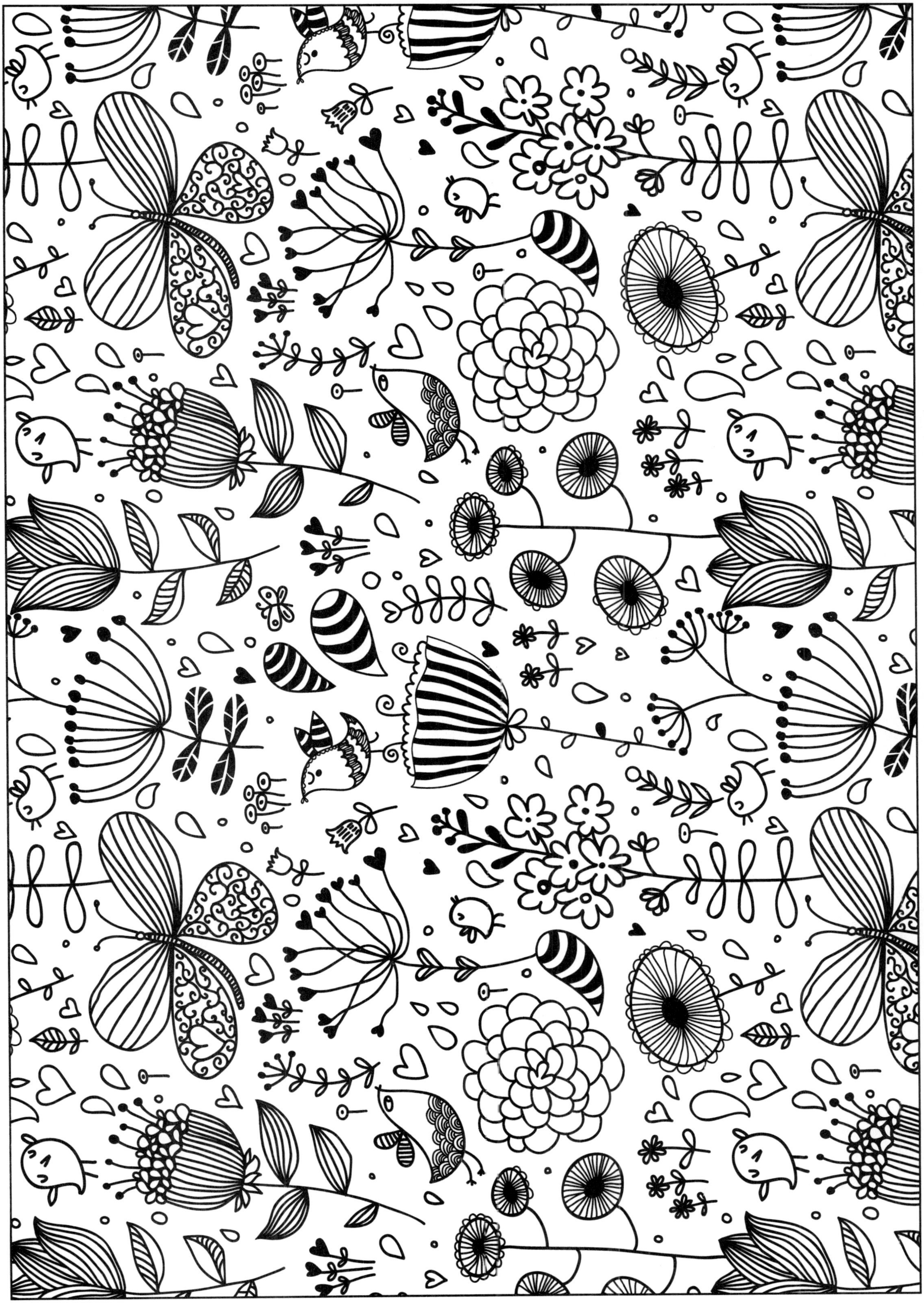

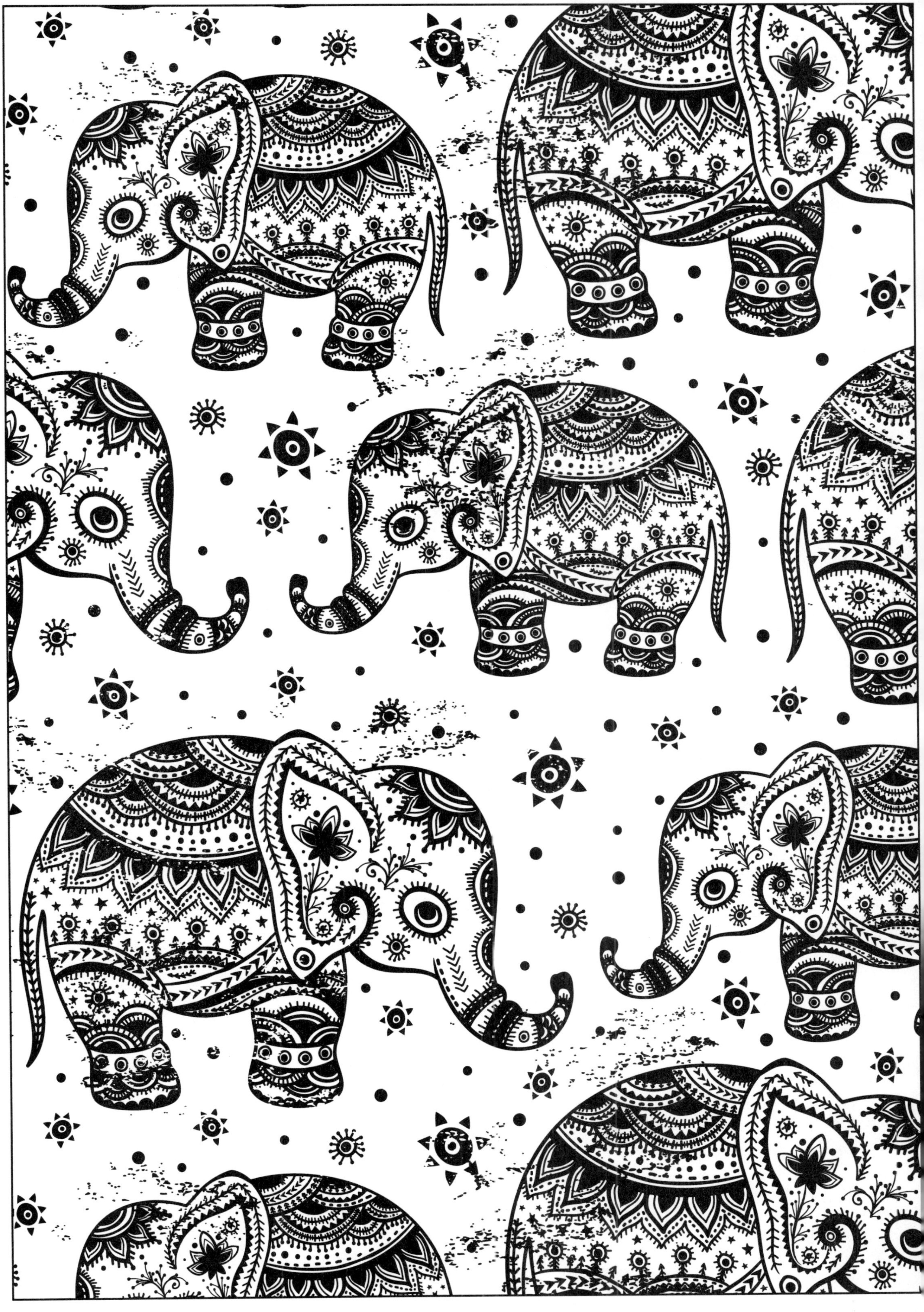

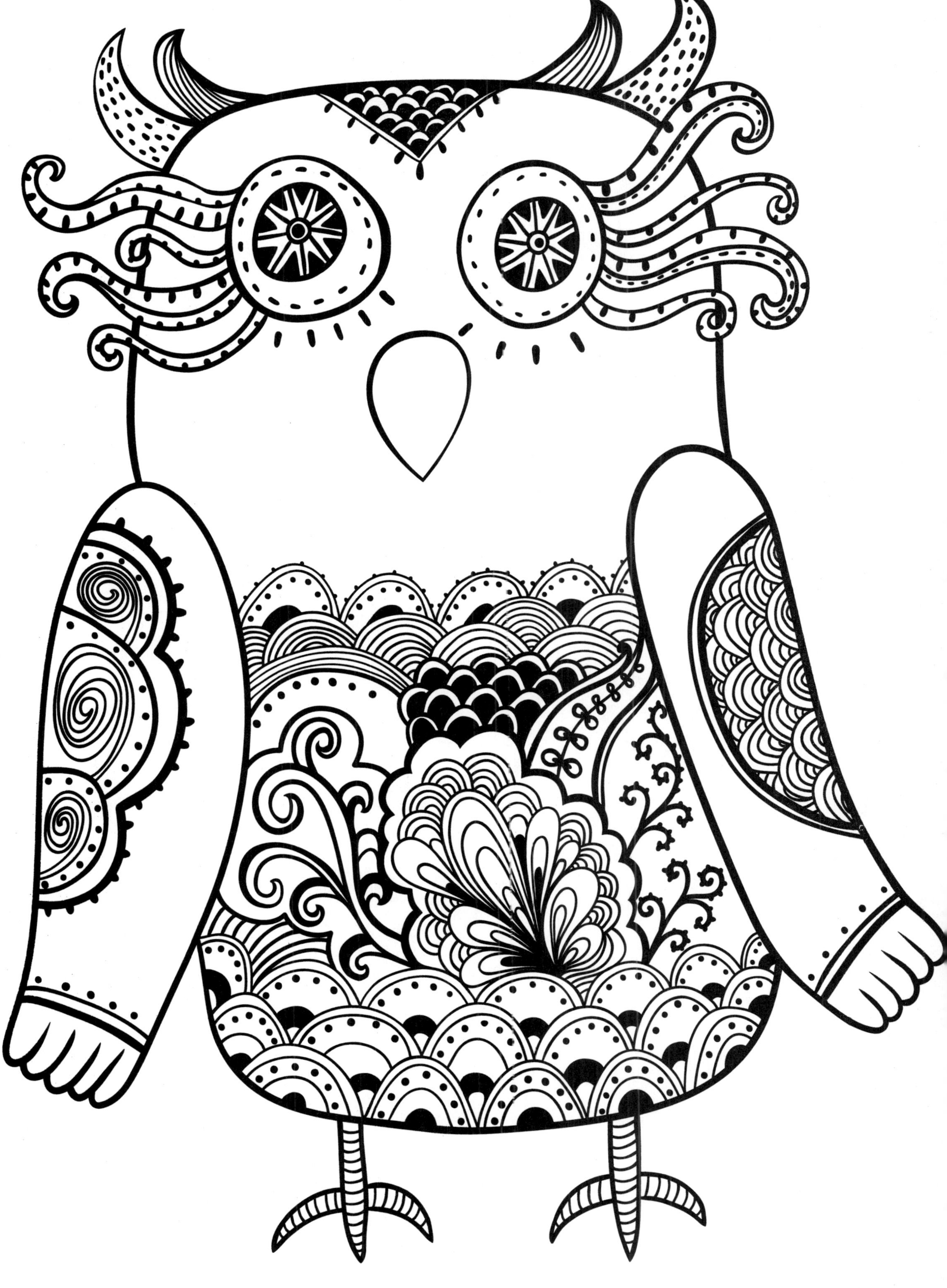

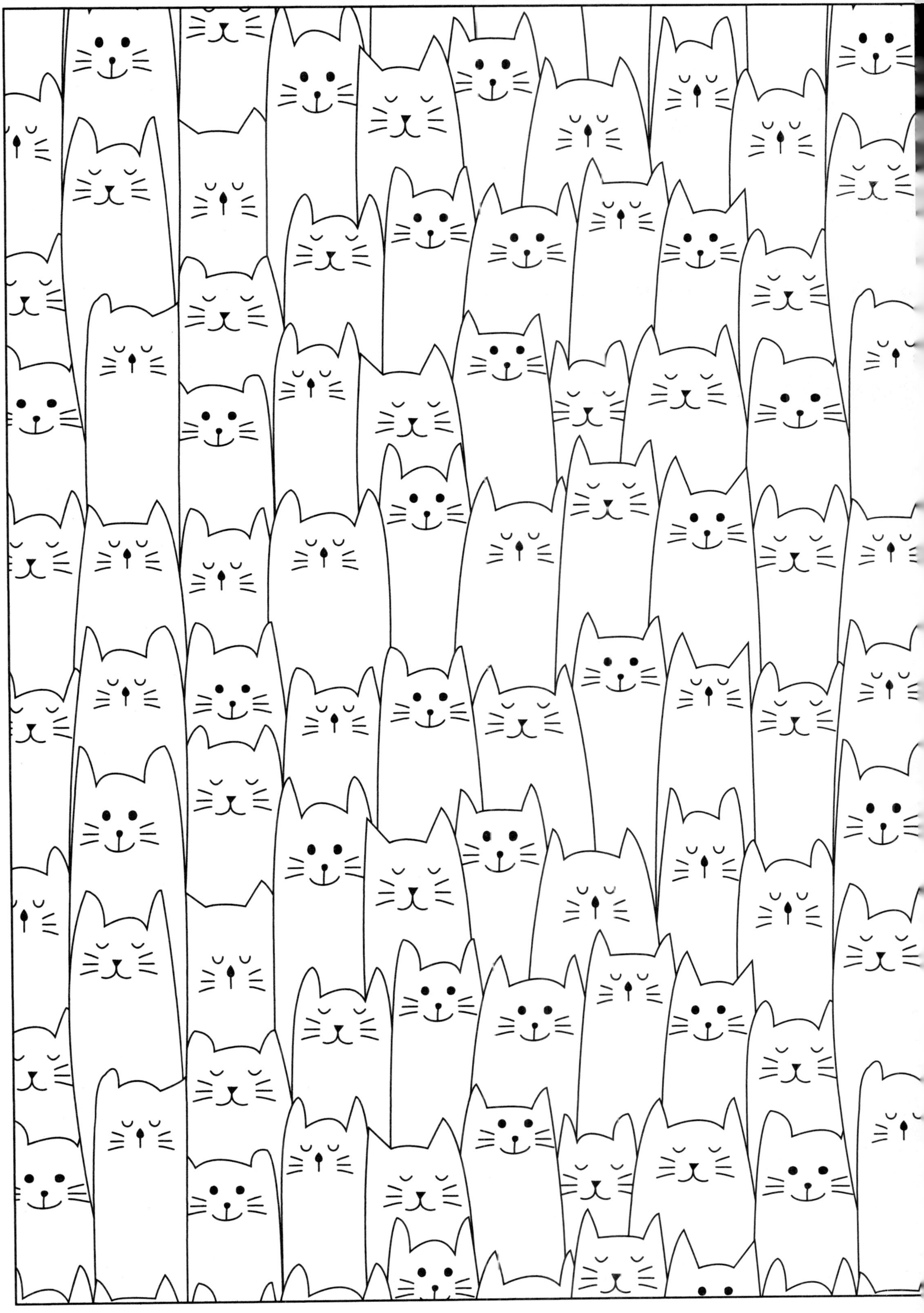

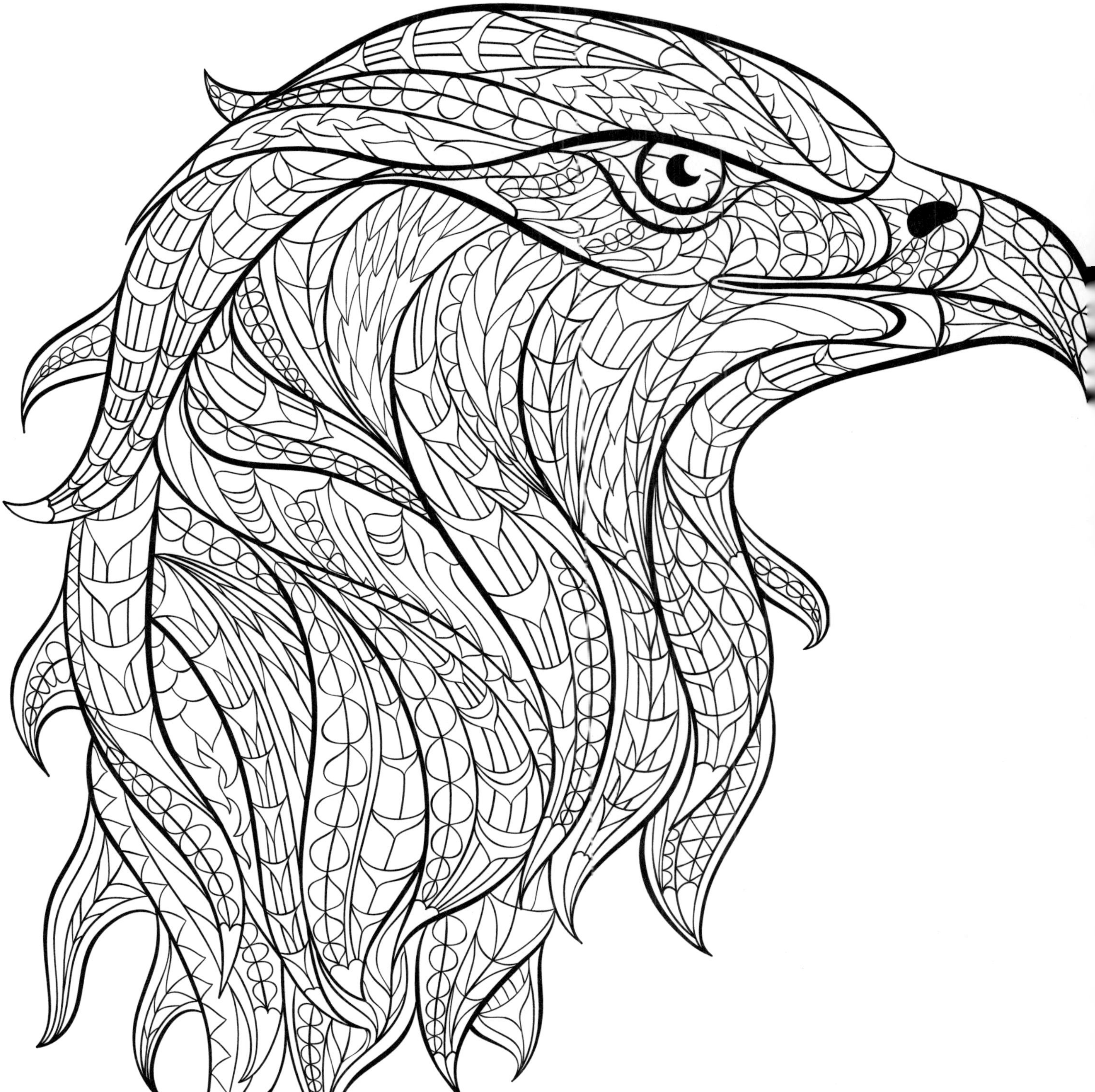

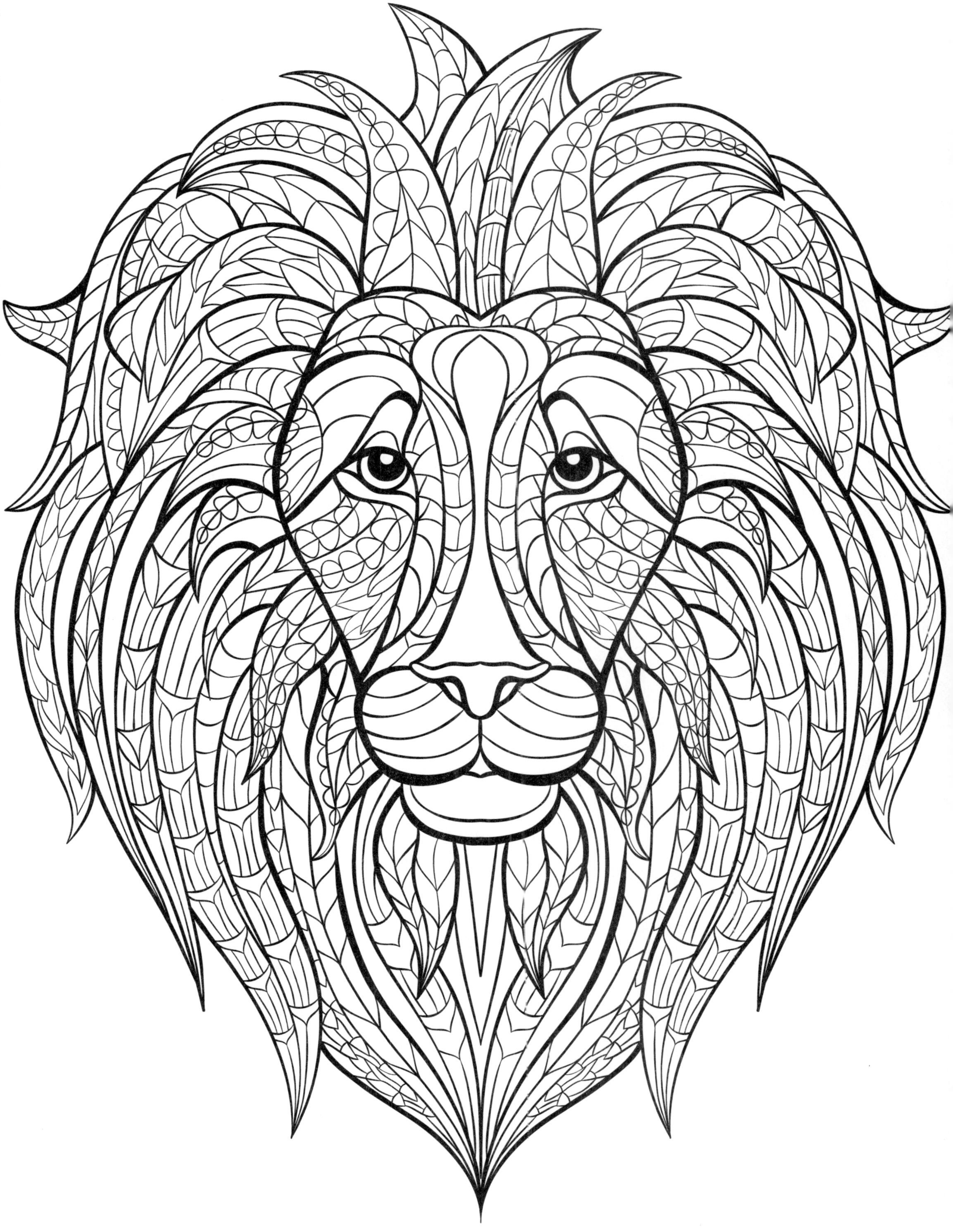

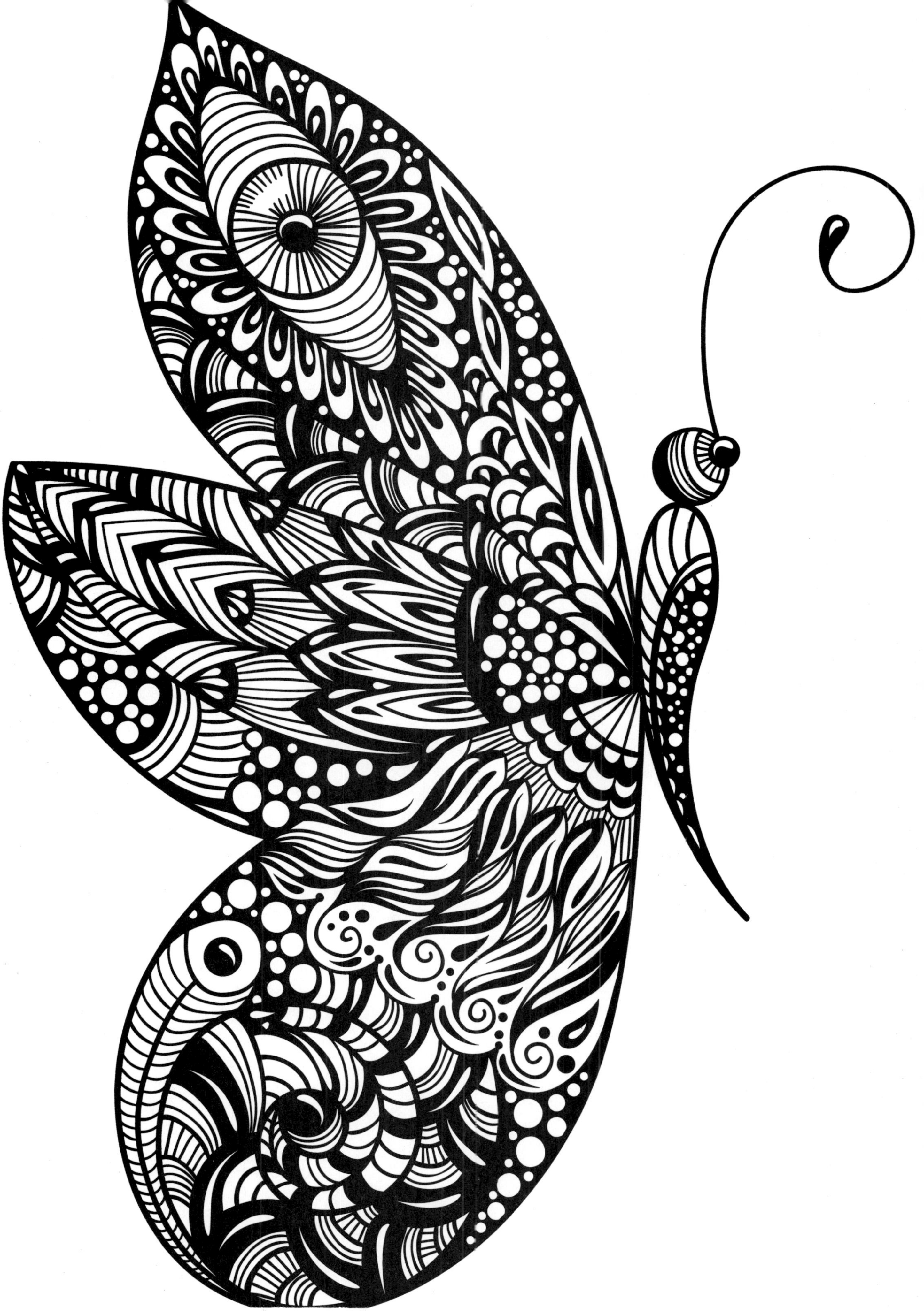

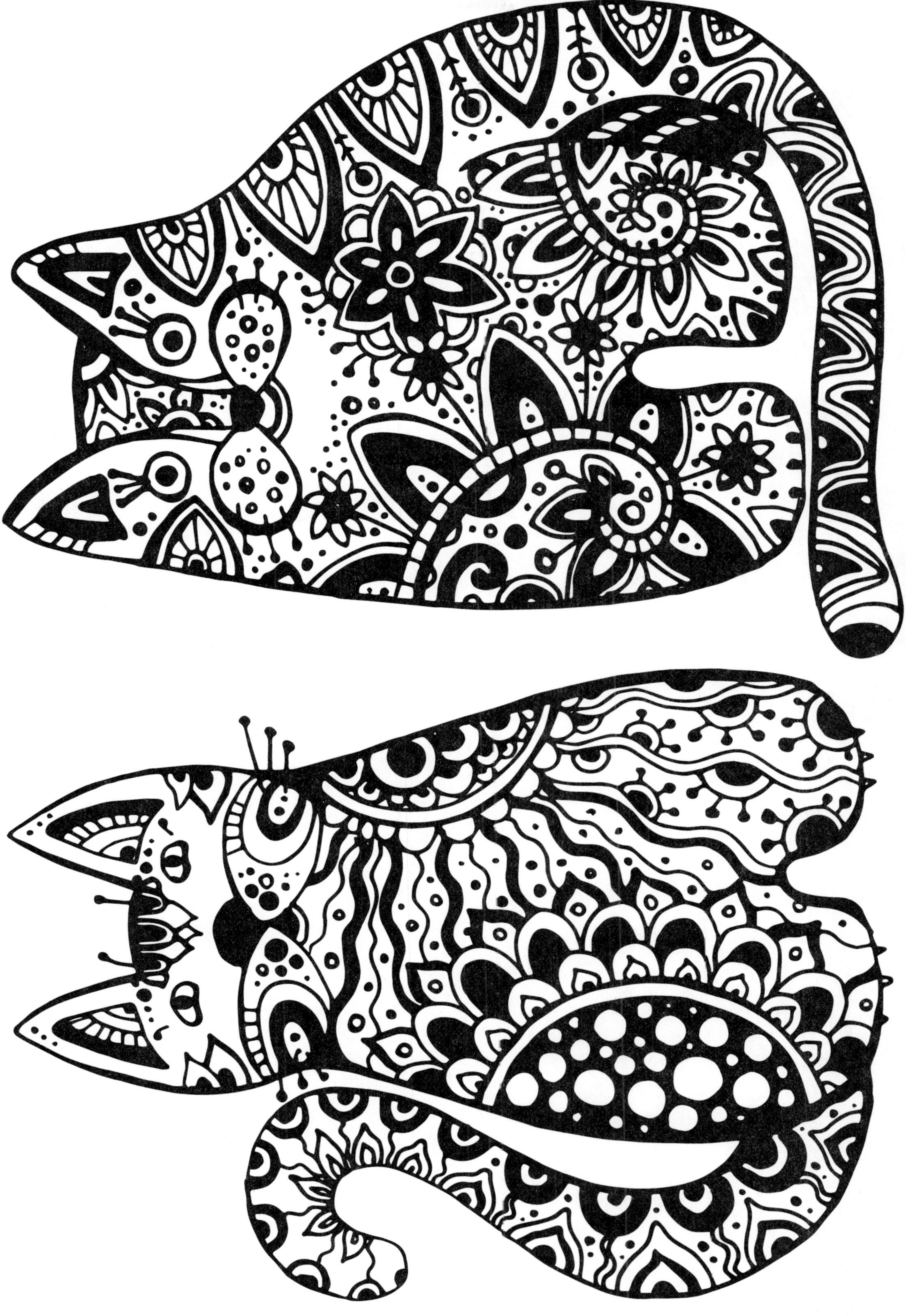

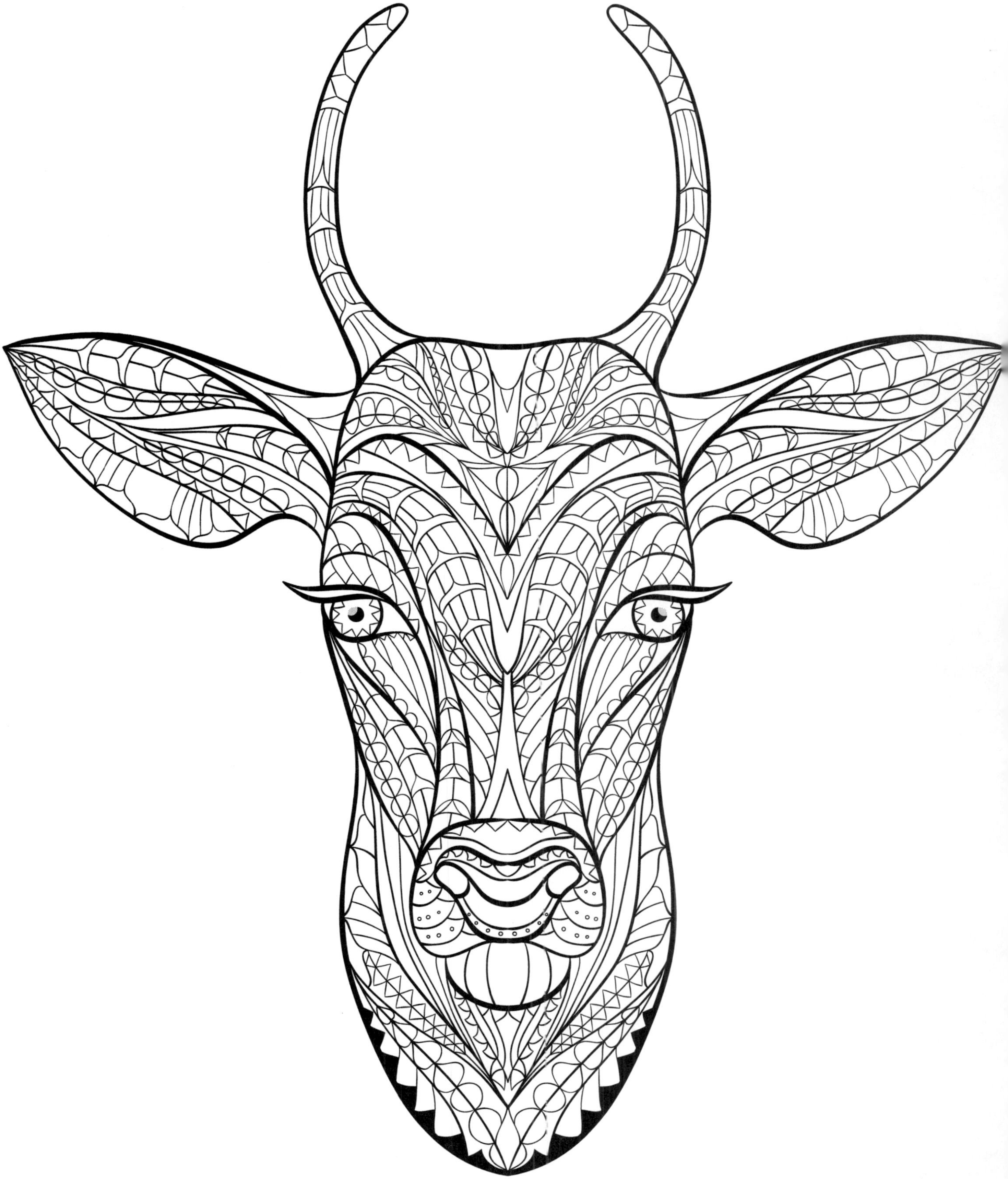

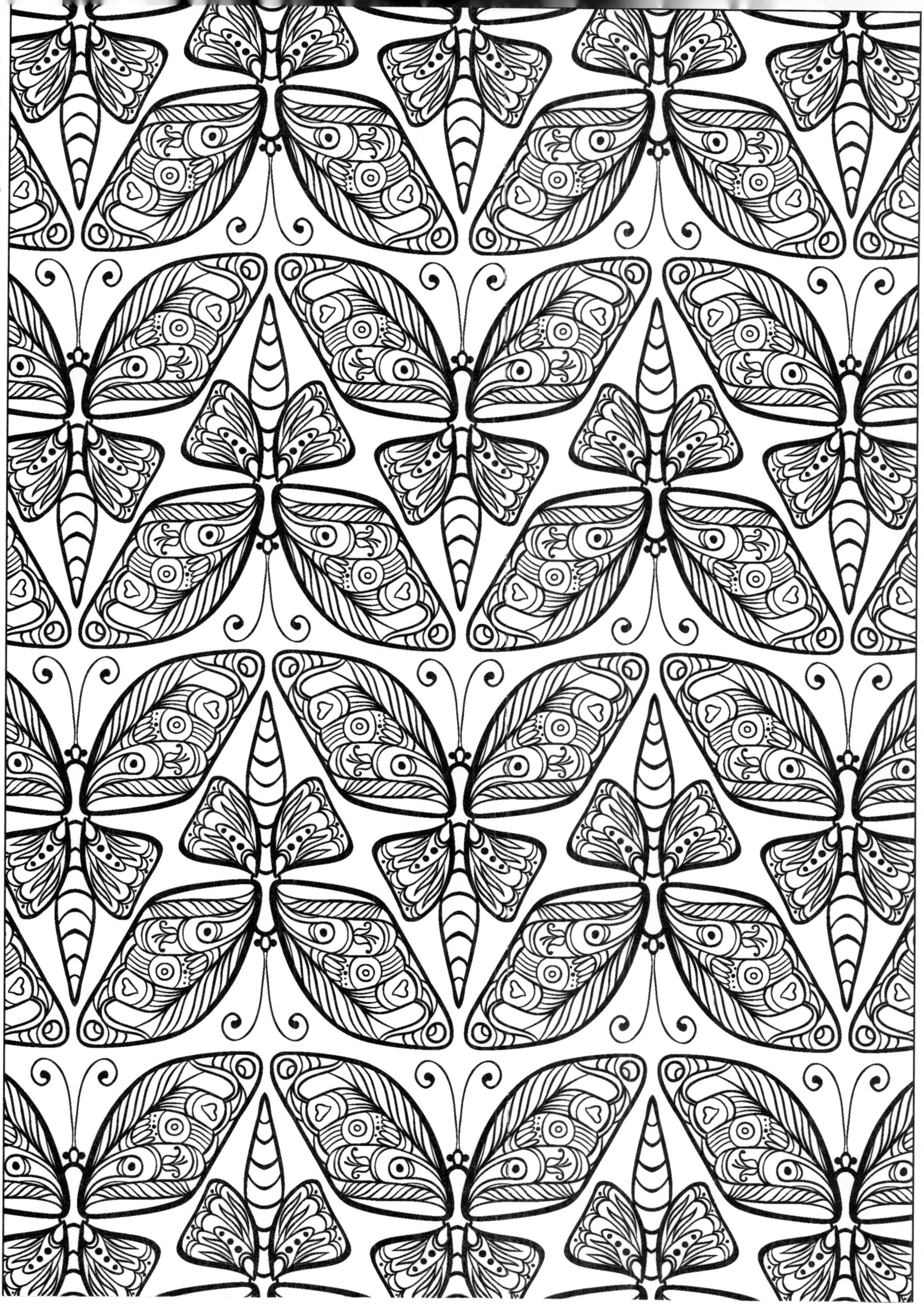

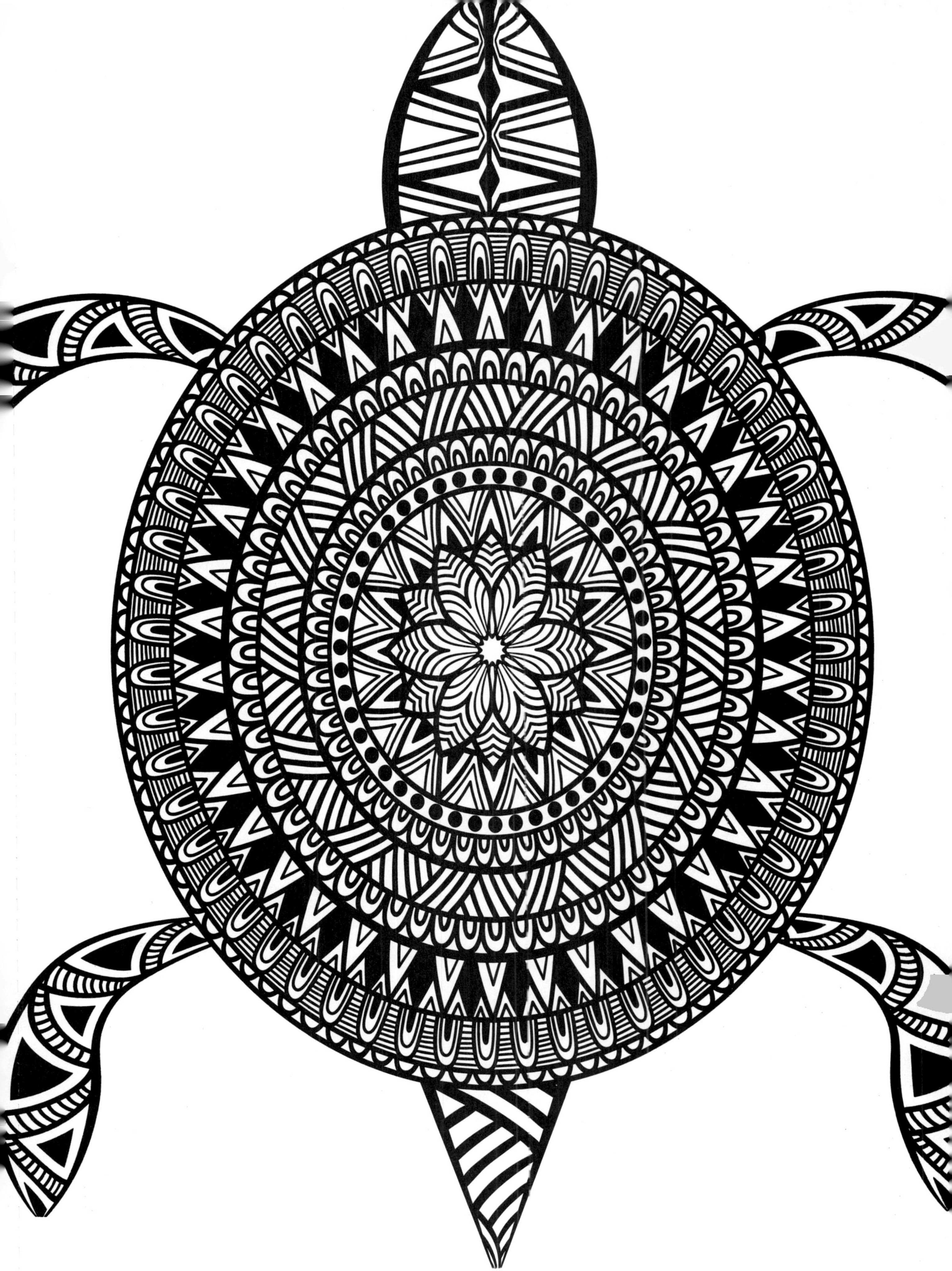

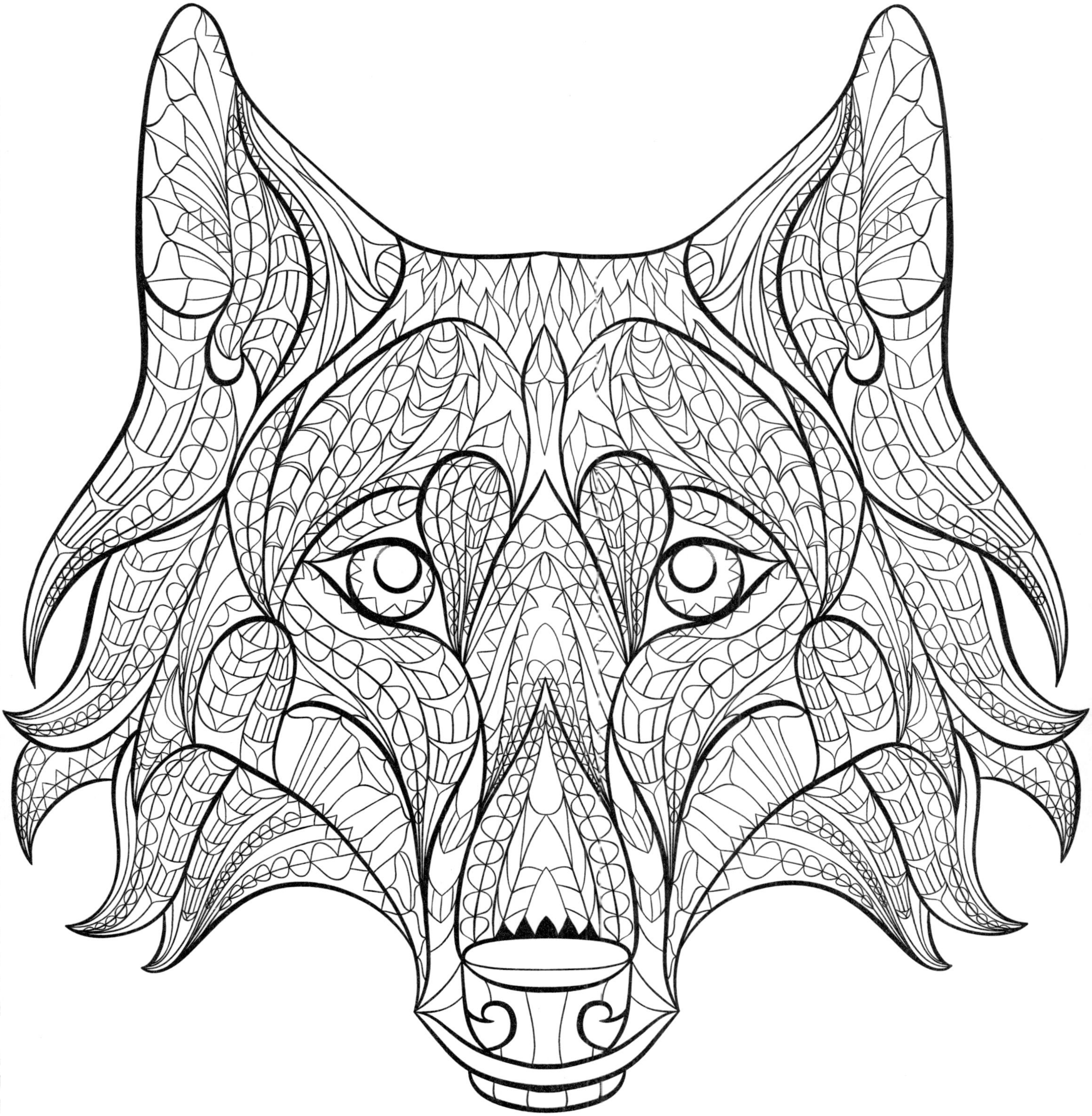

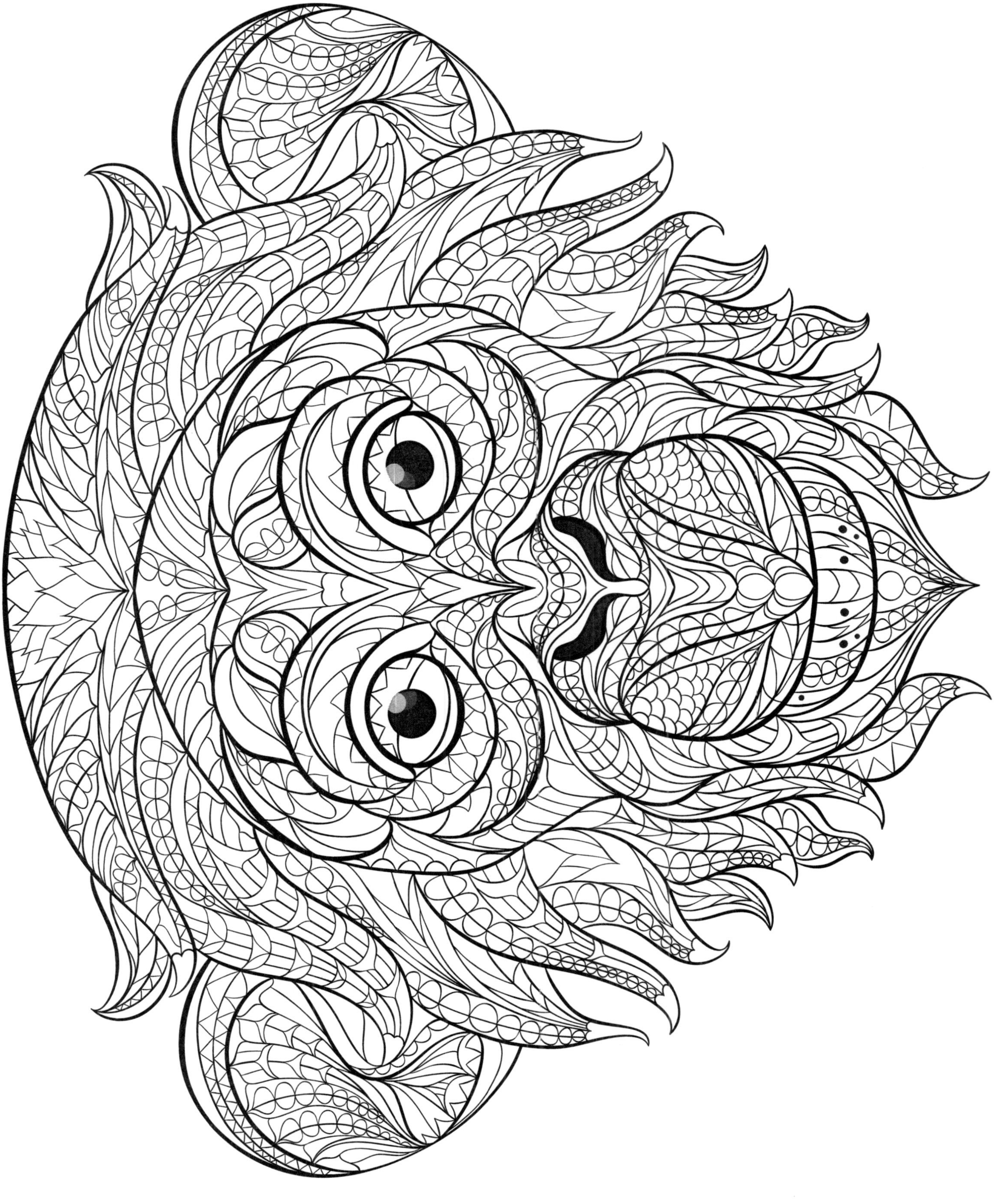

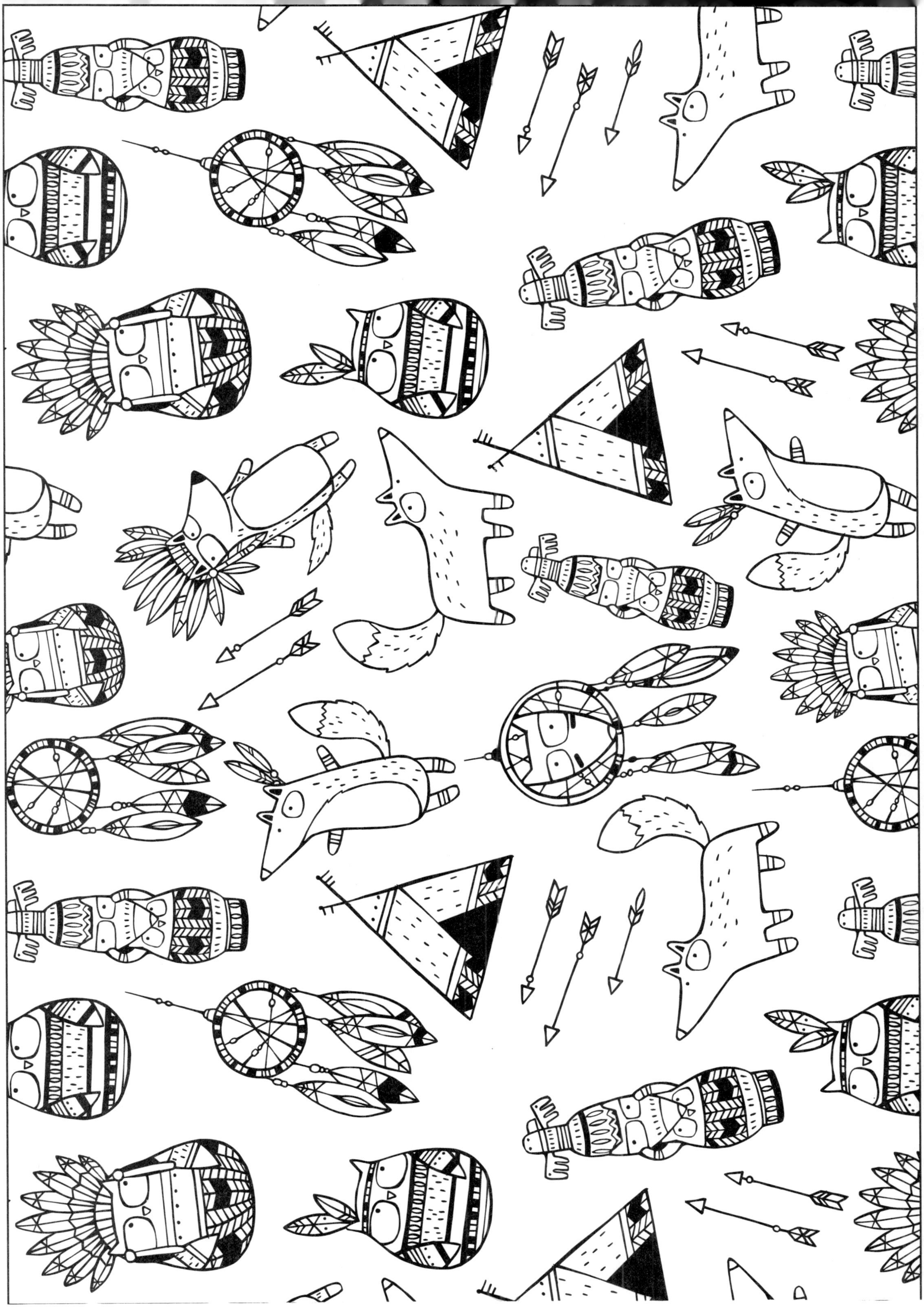

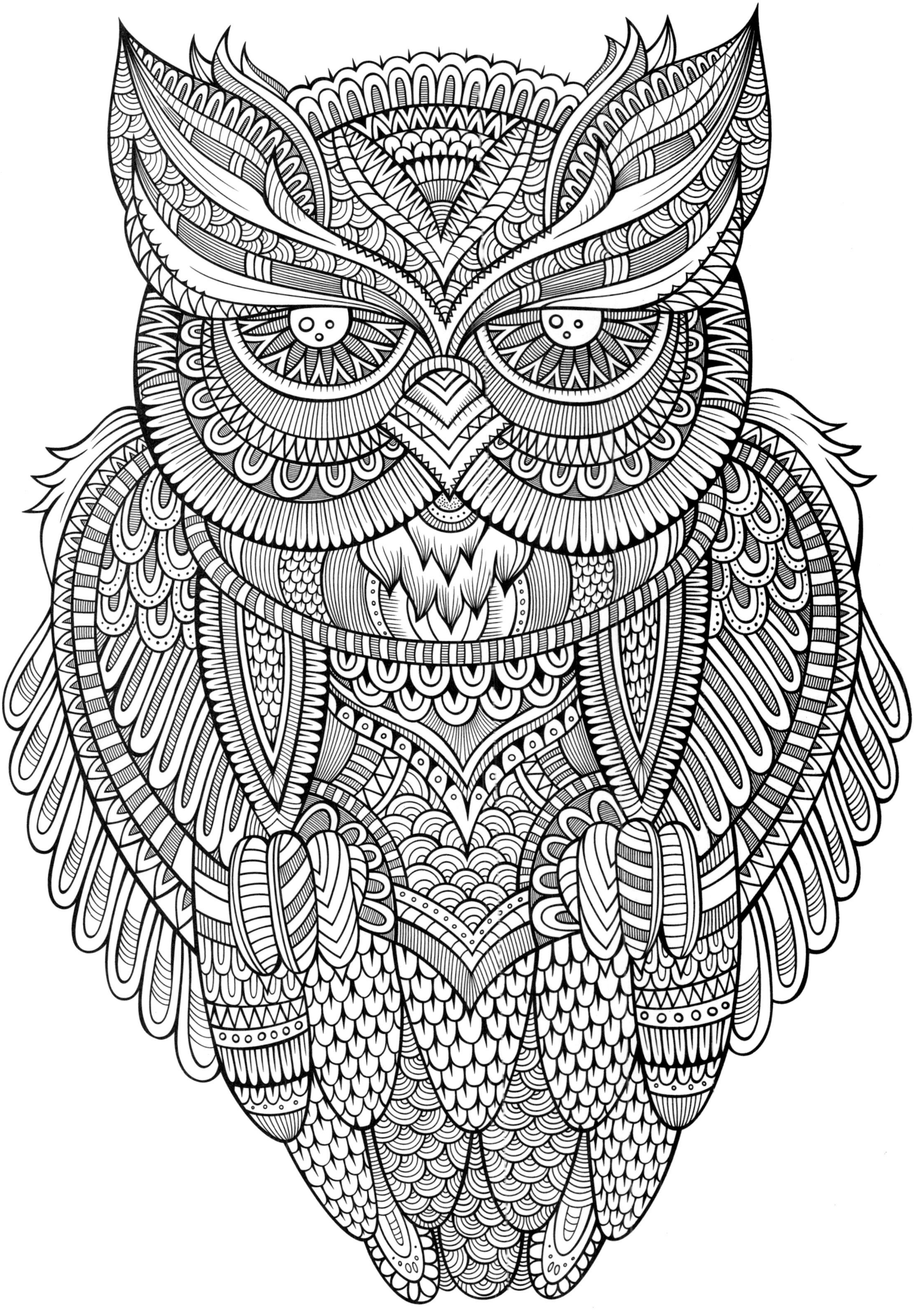

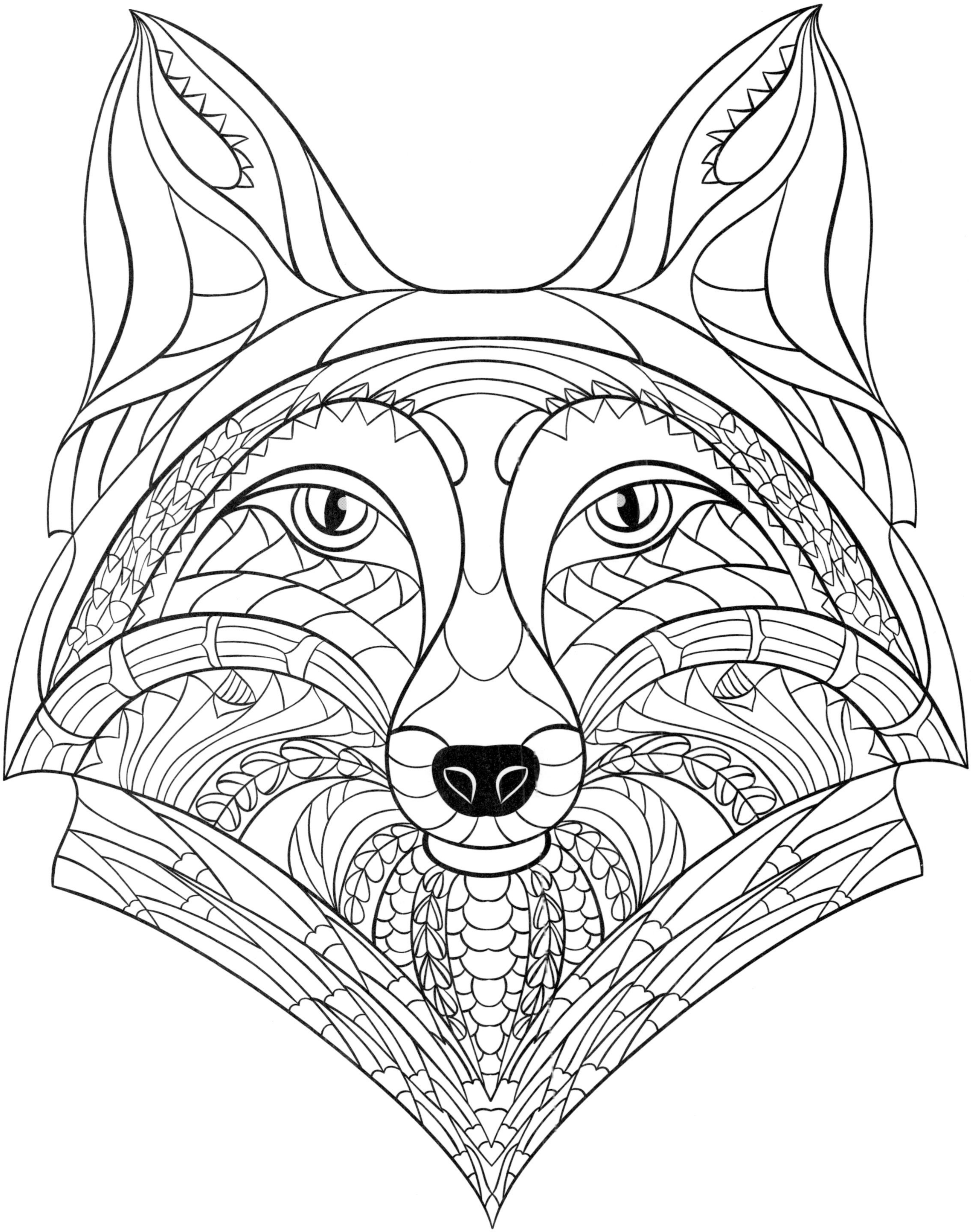

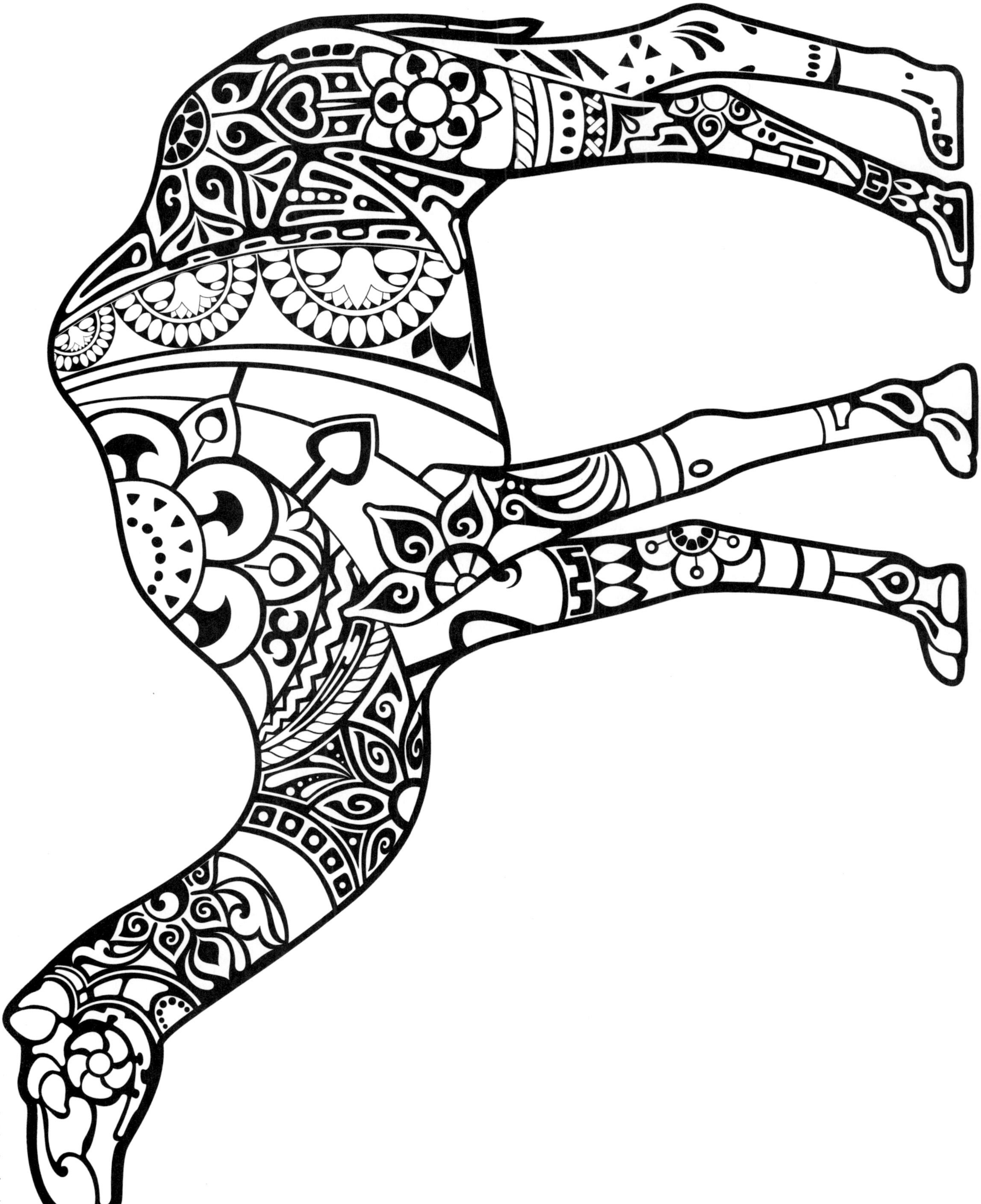

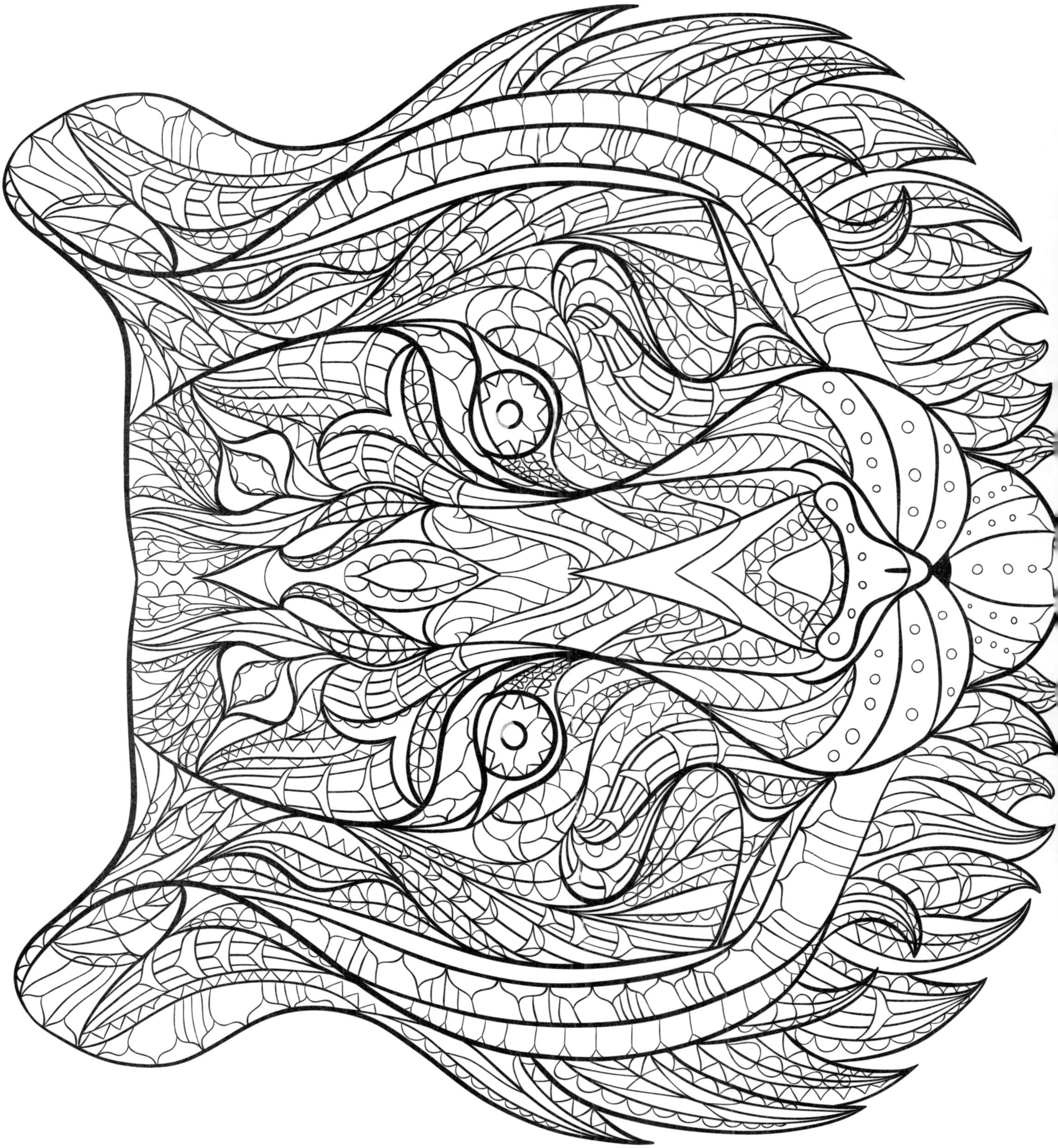

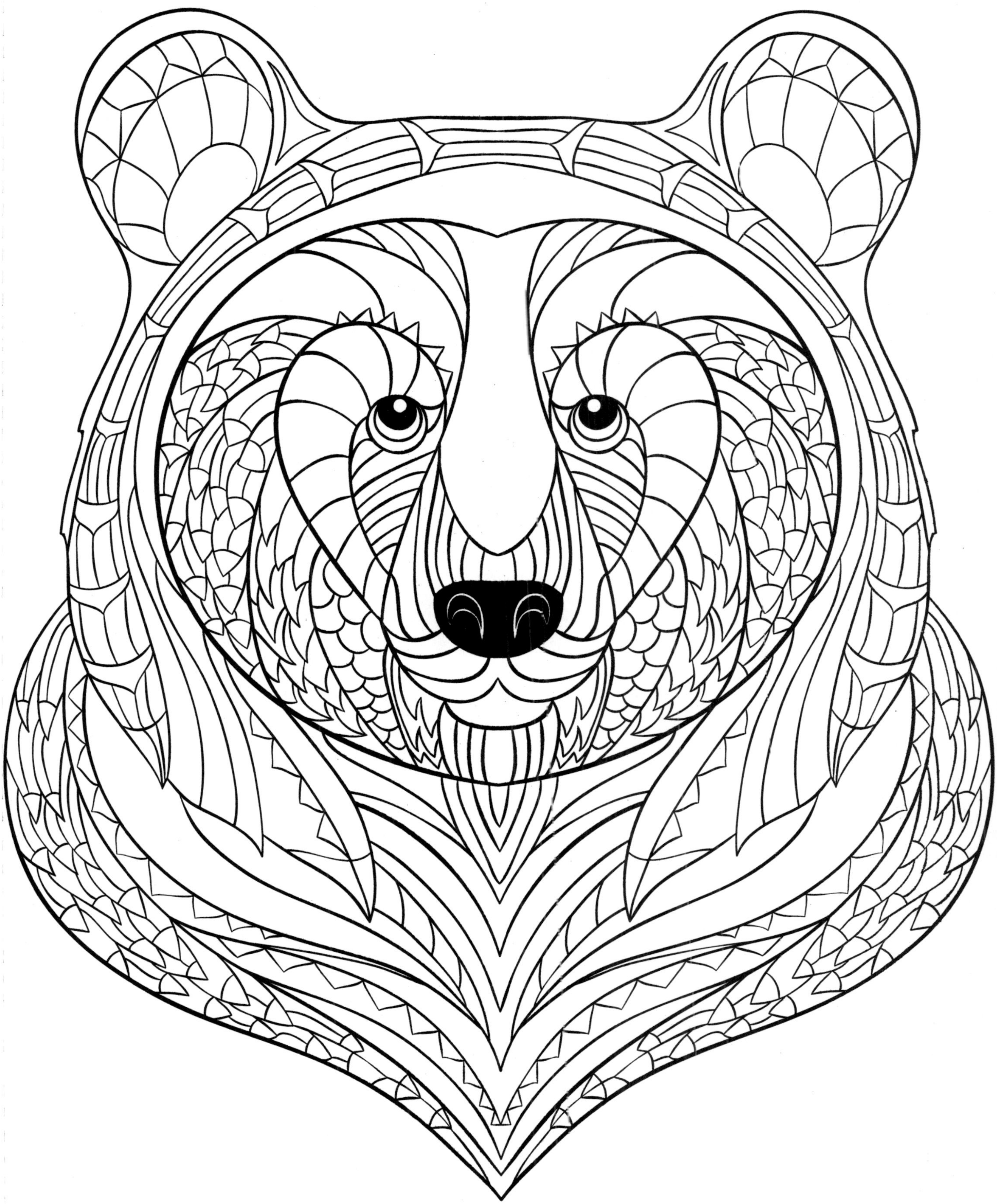

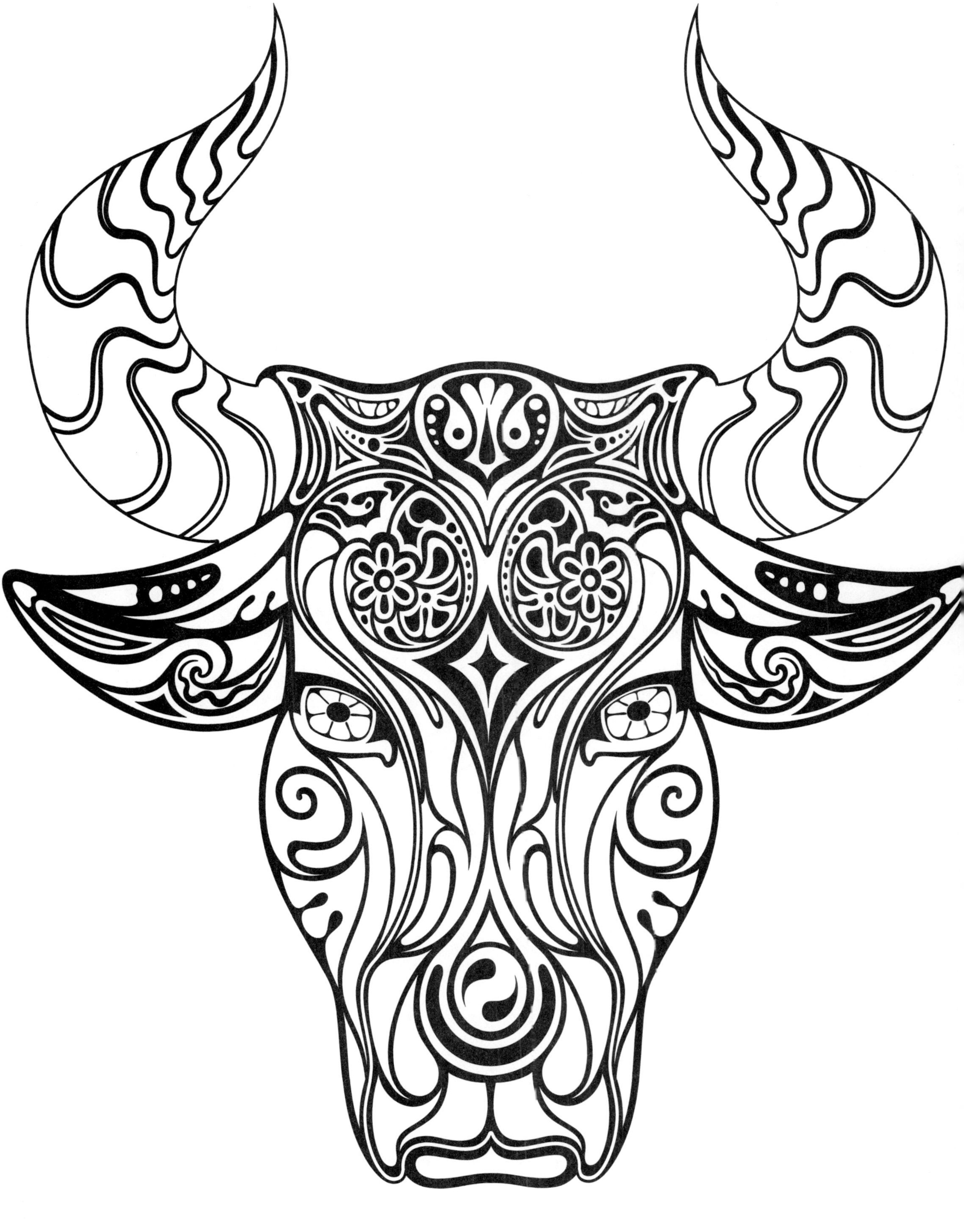

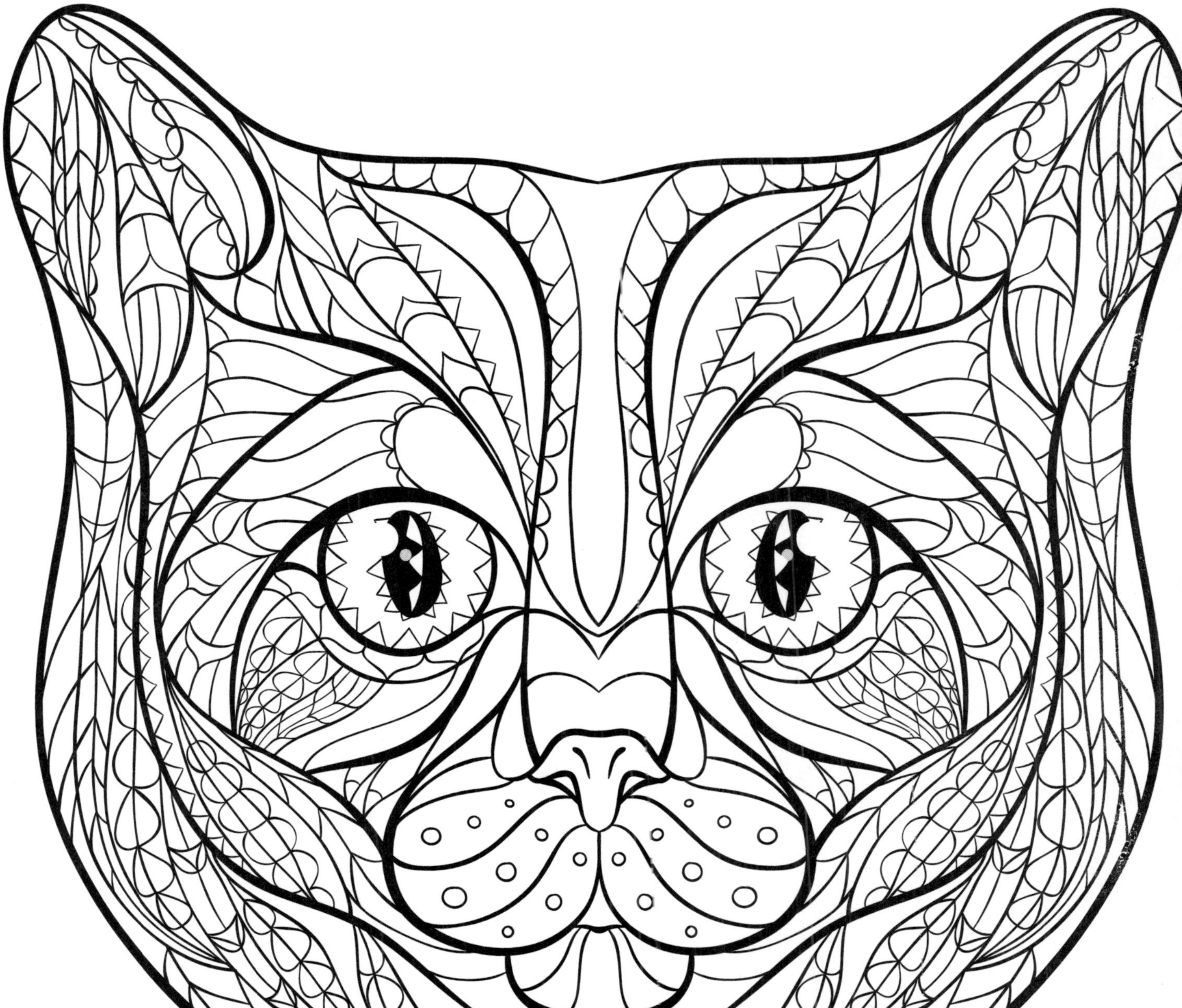

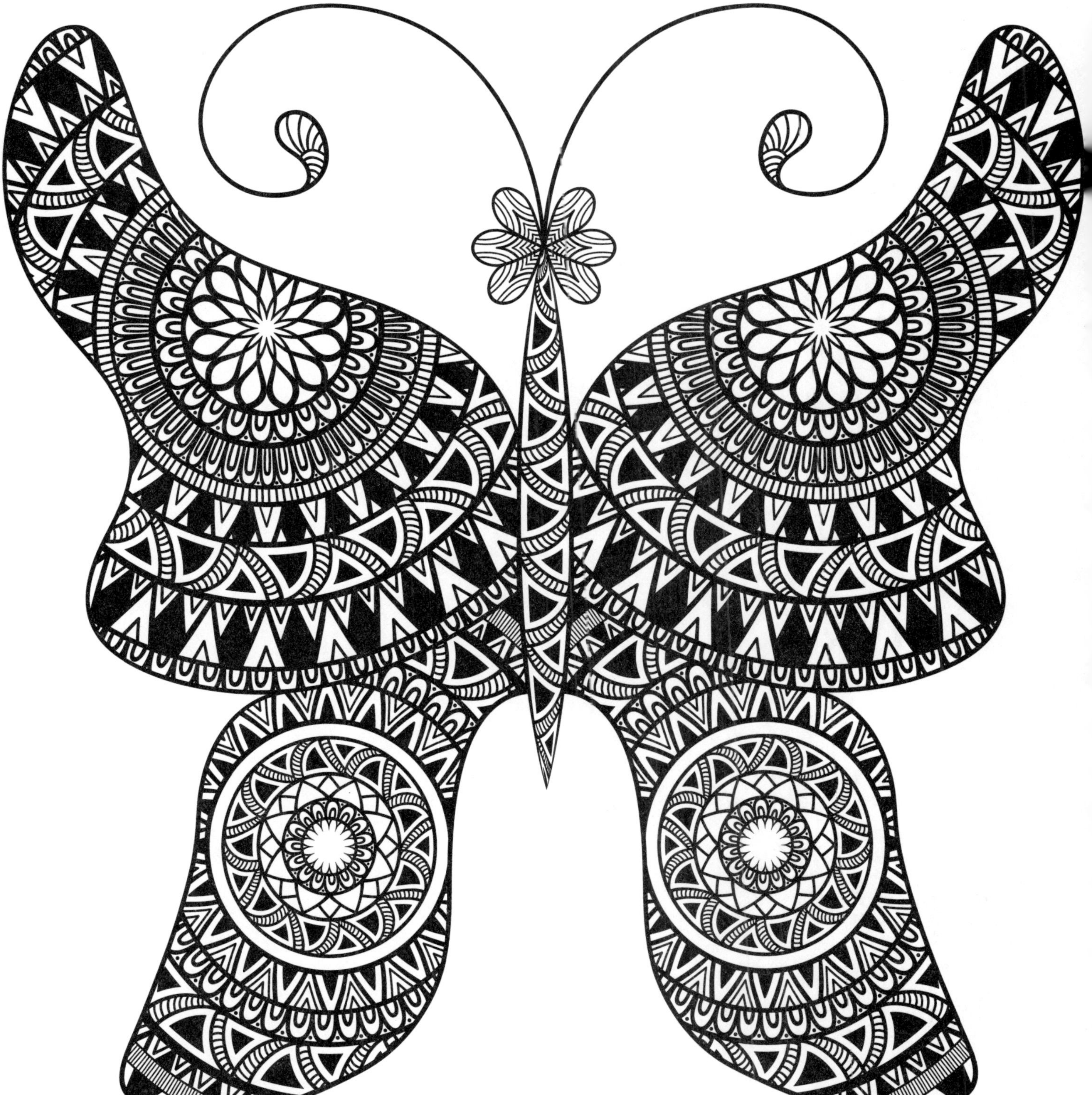

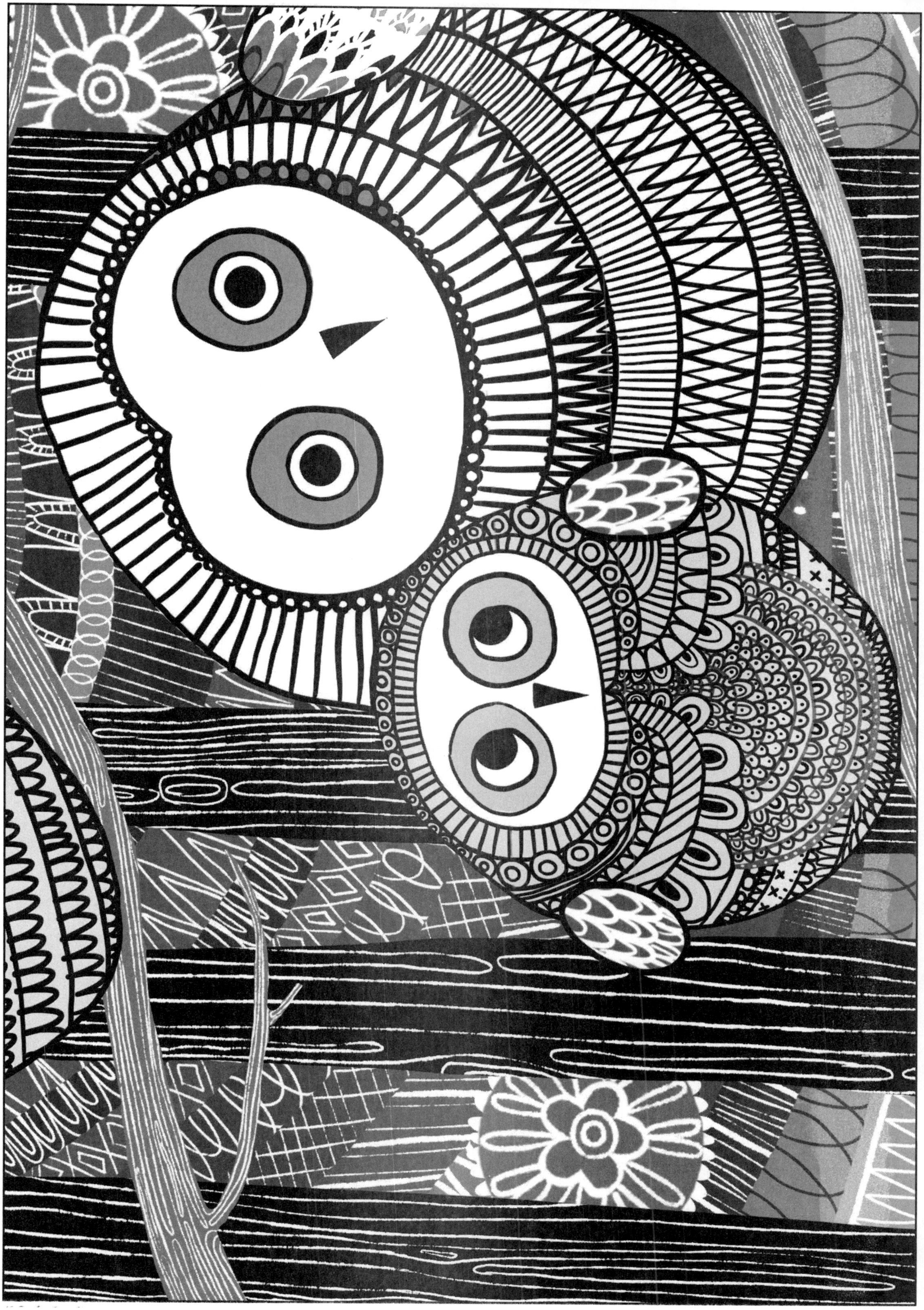

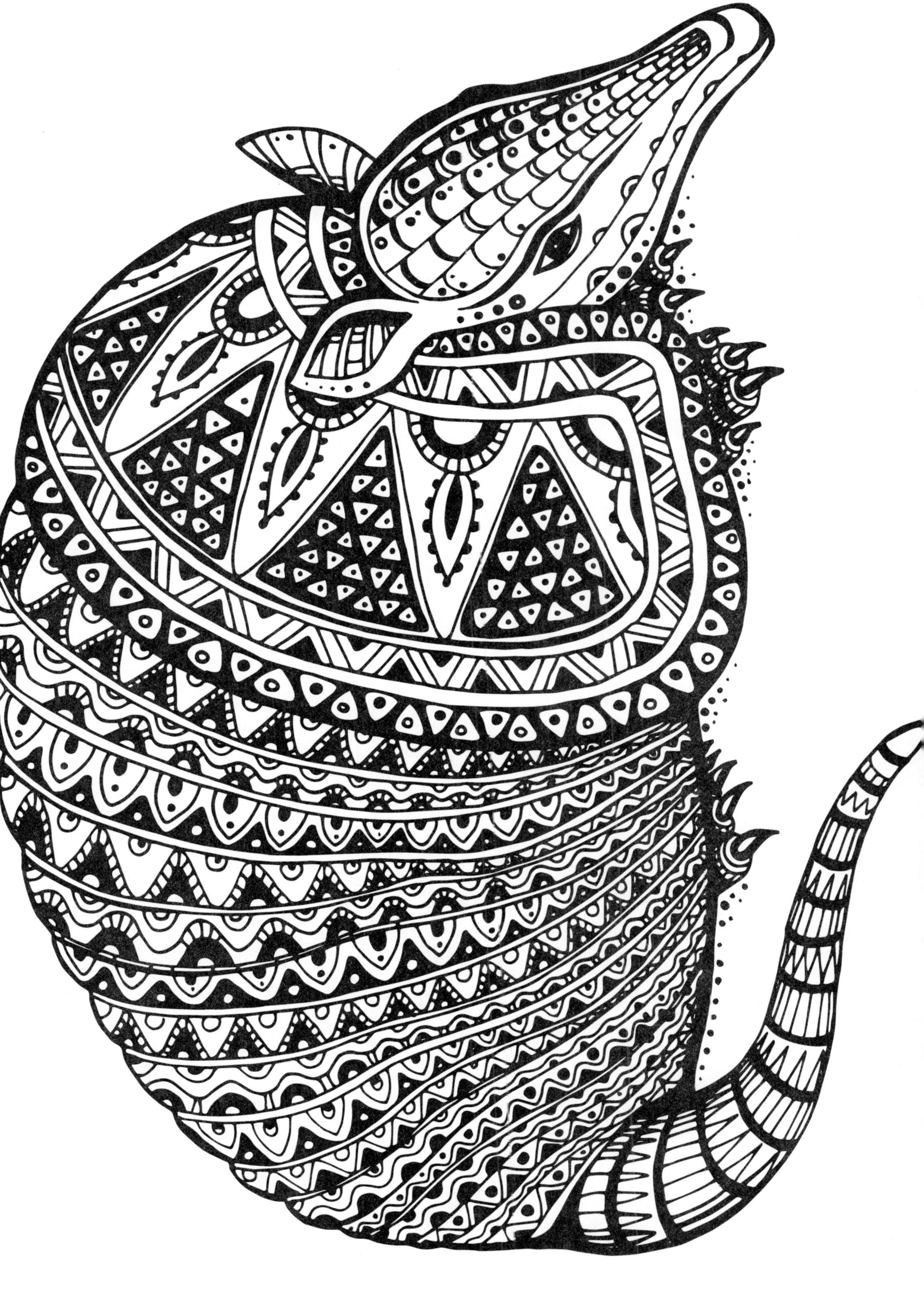

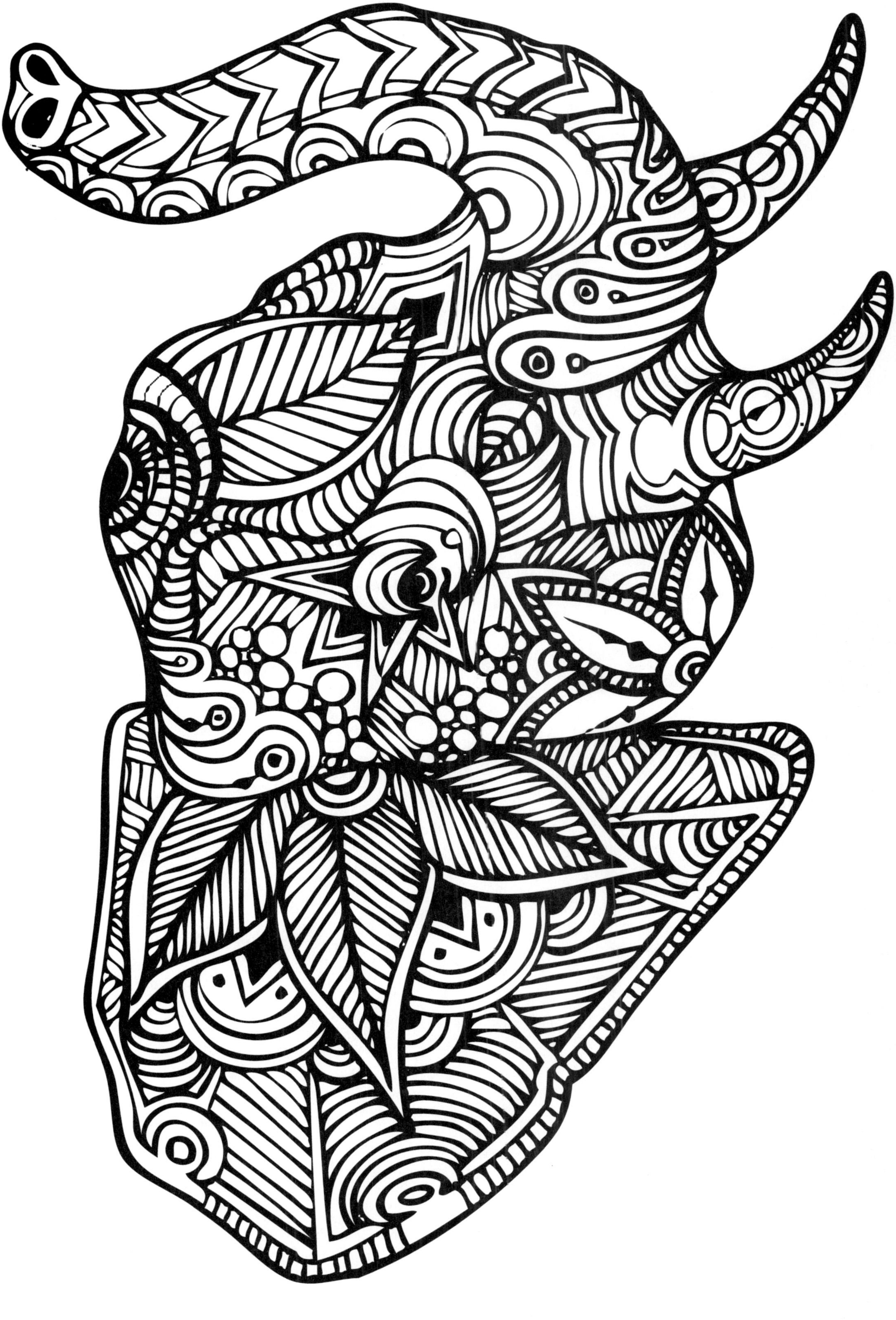

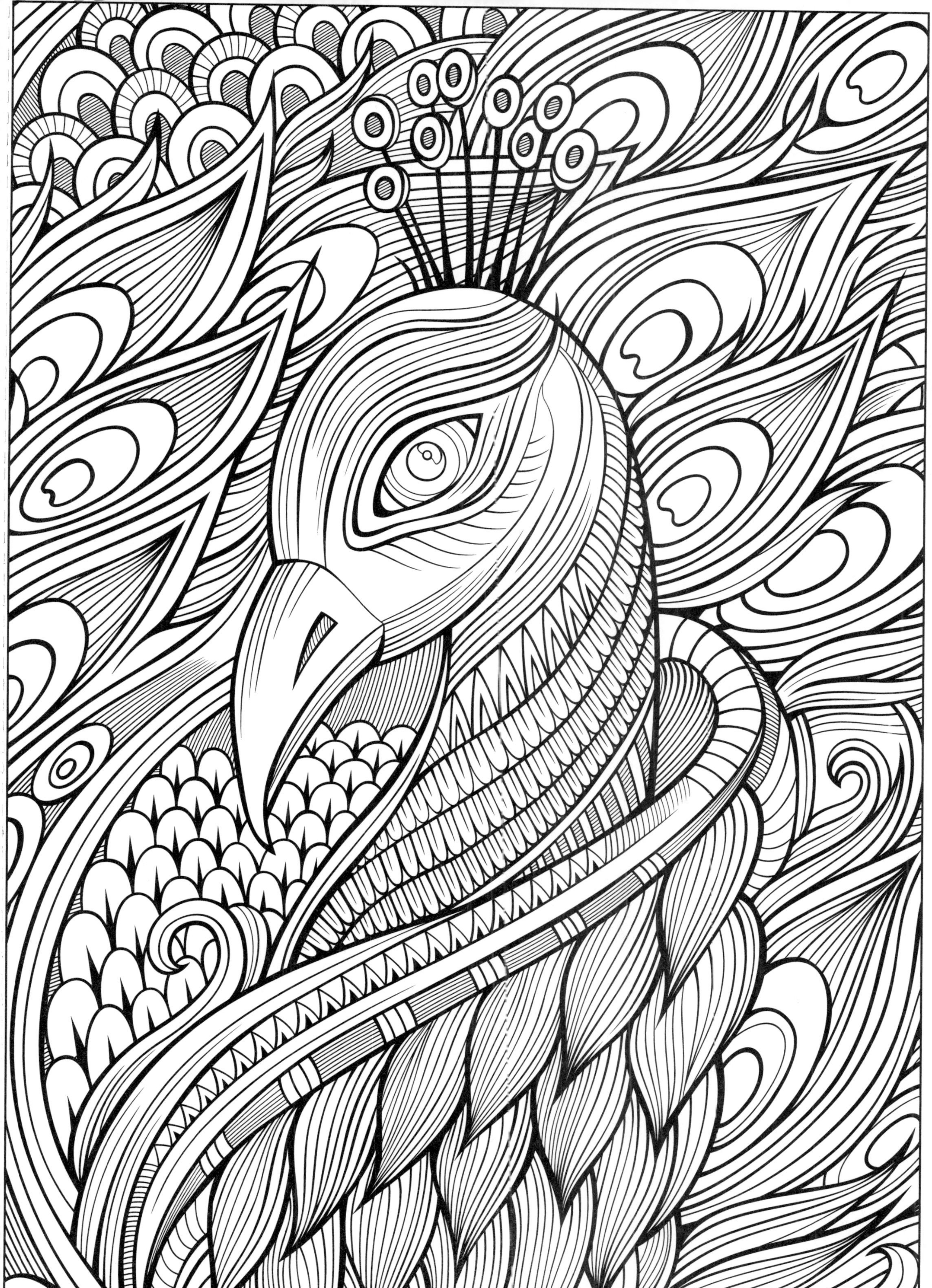